MW01686359

LIBERTY

THE LIFE AND TIMES OF AN ADVENTURER'S COMPANION

Jody –
Enjoy these adventures
as well as your own,
Carole Genaro
8-10-19

Carole Genaro

LIBERTY
THE LIFE AND TIMES OF
AN ADVENTURER'S COMPANION

First Printing 2013 Mortimore Publishing, Lander, WY

ISBN 0-9721352-8-6
Printed in the United States of America

Mortimore Publishing
805 Mortimore lane
Lander WY 82520

Dedication

To my Agency "buddies" for all the encouragement and reinforcement that helped me explore and enjoy new country, new activities and new experiences:

Skip Shoutis - Shoshone National Forest Back Country Ranger

Ray Hanson - Bureau of Land Management recreation planner

Tom Oliff - Yellowstone National Park Back country Trails Coordinator

Table of Contents

Acknowledgements

I can not thank enough all the help and support I have received to complete this project. I apologize for anyone I may miss, but please know that even if I have failed to mention you in these acknowledgements, your efforts are greatly appreciated.

Katherine, who helped me learn basic computer skills to be able to use a recently acquired laptop to document the stories.

Kyle, my computer "geek" who kept me sane and inspired me to continue with the effort after he retrieved my "lost" material multiple times from the bowels of the laptop.

Tony, Sherry, Carol and all the others who contributed to the "magic" along the journey for which I am so grateful.

Ray, the outfitter who opened doors through which I passed to enjoy the journey.

Shelly and Brandy, who both went the distance with me.

Patty Trautman, another "horse lover" who read, edited and critiqued my manuscripted stories to make them more readable and for the inspiration with my chapter titles.

Roz Westman for subtitle concepts and for putting it all together that others might also enjoy the journey.

1

THE FIRST YEARS

It all started with kicking, biting, and plain ornery behavior. A friend even said to me, "Carole, be careful with this one, he could hurt you bad". My friend, Johnny, had brought this registered buckskin horse colt home for me in his 4 horse trailer. After being pushed against corral posts and poles, stepped on, and struck at with fast moving hoofs and flashing teeth, he had maneuvered the agitated animal with menacing dark eyes into position to secure its lead rope for the ride down the road to a new home.

His home had been a box stall with periodic freedom of a board fence runway that led to the arena. The year and a half colt had reportedly cleared the high board entrance at least twice. Daily lunging on a long line helped curb his high energy and athletic urges.

His owner was the sister of the caretaker of the fair grounds where he was kept. The girl had also owned his mother. When the mare had to be put down because of a broken leg from a cattle guard accident, the girl began training the colt with the intent of replacing his mother for barrel racing and other rodeo activities. His outbursts and obnoxious behavior didn't show much potential. The horse could be handled by her, but intensively rebelled against any direction from a man. She put out the word he was for sale at a reasonable price.

As a young girl, I had dreamed of going to California, marrying a cowboy, and raising horses. Here I was, living in Wyoming, married to sort-of-a cowboy, and had horses. My registered quarter horse mare, Babe, was half of an equation...I would look for the other half.

One day 30 years ago, a friend stopped by to tell me about a horse I might be interested in looking at. I went to see him. Talk about fitting the bill! He was a young, beautiful, muscular, registered stud colt. His buckskin coat rippled with dark highlights. I was entranced with him. After a brief visit with his owner, a deal was made and I left to make arrangements to get him home. I knew I had my work cut out for me, little did I know.

The colt's temporary new home was a pole corral in my dirt floored "garage". The first times I approached him, he showed his displeasure with the new accommodations. He didn't want anything to do with me. When he finally gave into some curiosity about me, I rewarded him with a bucket of water which he promptly drank from and tipped over. Positive behavior was necessary to receive a bite of hay. He progressed to smelling my hand, then my touching his nose. We were getting acquainted! Soon after, I was able to get a lead rope on him, which was followed by short walks in my very small pasture. He still attempted to go his own direction, which often amounted to anywhere but where I was going. After a couple days we had progressed to lunging and some good responses to starting, stopping, and direction of movement. He and I were making progress.

A couple of weeks passed and I decided he was ready for introduction to his future "lady". Babe was in a nearby pasture of about 3 acres. Hurriedly I opened the gate, lead him in, closed the gate, and took off the lead rope. Catching sight of Babe, he raced toward her with loud calls. Several times each following day, I would drive along the fence on the side road. The colt would be doing laps around the perimeter of the pasture, often herding his lady ahead of him. Mane and tail flying, I often felt tears on my cheeks as he rejoiced in this new freedom. What joy I felt for him!

Babe's breeding had LEO blood in it. Liberty's registered name was KING LIBERTY BARS. There were possibilities for fine colts. I had had Babe for a number of years and at sight or sound of me or one of my vehicles, she would come. If she was out of hearing range of my voice, a few toots of the horn would bring her in. This confused Liberty at first but soon he was approaching hesitantly, cued by her trusting behavior. He learned this could be rewarded by a tasty treat, bite of hay, pat on the neck, maybe a feel good scratch. Still he continued to be mostly stand-offish.

Even though I never witnessed any outright breeding between the two, he got the job done. The following spring Babe proudly brought her bay filly to me. I called her Missy. Her American Quarter Horse Association registered name would be FILLY BARLEO. Liberty was a sire at the age of three.

During the following winter, I got a phone call telling me there was an extra horse in my pasture. When I arrived, I saw Babe protecting her baby, and Liberty trying desperately to protect his family, amidst much kicking, biting, and chasing. With a friend's (soon to be husband's) help, the intruder was gotten out of the pasture and Babe was looked over. She had some bloody discharge and some bloody mess was found on the ground nearby. She was loaded into the trailer and taken to the vet where we learned she had possibly been carrying twins. Thankfully, a live fetus appeared to be okay. Liberty had minor bites and dings. During the following weeks, he allowed me to clean and treat them, though with great apprehension. More trust was apparent.

The weather moderated as we waited for another foal. We were ever so thankful early one morning to see a shaky but healthy sorrel colt attempting to master standing up, encouraged by his doting mom. Sister and Dad stood nearby as curious as could be. In the next few days, Babe again brought her baby to me for approval. DUSTY BOY BARLEO was also accepted for registration.

In the past as well as the future, I learned hard lessons about raising colts, and horses in general. My vet advised me not to breed Babe again as she had shortness of breath, commonly known as the heaves, due to being fed dusty hay years earlier. Each colt was harder on her and another could take her life. He would geld Liberty right away. Dusty was weaned from his mother and kept separate so he could hopefully grow more before being gelded. His small but compact and perfectly proportioned body could use any help available.

Time passed, during which I spent many hours working with all of my horse family. I began to notice something different about Liberty's behavior when my (now) husband, Gary, was around. Liberty was more apt to hang back or not seem interested in what I was doing. When the girl I had bought him from had talked to me about his behavior, she had said that her brother couldn't do anything with him and really was convinced the horse didn't like him at all. Could it be possible he didn't like men in general? Although I felt he was okay with me, there was still an odd nagging feeling that we really hadn't "bonded".

Gary and I both enjoyed fishing and camping, and we decided we would try taking the horses for a days outing in the forest on South Pass. We had taken the horses for a few hours ride several times in and around Hudson and felt confident about our choice of places to begin our "horse trips". It turned into an overnight camping which included his son, Cody (7), and my daughter, Robin (8). After a fun experience and no major problems, we were ready to try a more involved outing.

We would do a weekend trip to Shoshone Lake from Dickinson Park. I poured over maps, bought and repackaged food items, decided what and what not to take, while Gary took care of the arrangements for hauling the horses, camping and fishing gear, and such. We took off down the road with much anticipation of a great experience.

Surveying our saddling and tacking up results, I think we must have looked like the "Beverly Hillbillies", only horseback! One adult, one child, two sleeping bags, food and clothes bags, fishing gear, picket pin and rope, leg hobble, and miscellaneous items on EACH horse. Also, my daughter was perched high on the tent on the back of my saddle. I had worked with both horses ahead of time to figure out how to tie everything on, just not with both of us on, too. Robin had ridden double with me several times, so it was just a matter of me getting my leg over everything and her clambering on. Gary and Cody were on and we were on our way.

Soon after leaving the trailhead, a long "boardwalk" goes across a boggy meadow. I held my breath until we reached the end of it; a step off either side would be disastrous. As we hopped off the end and followed Babe to the right, Liberty picked this point in time and place to try bucking even though he had not really ever bucked with me before. The only thing we had going for us was the amount of stuff on him. "Hang on tight, Robin"! A few hops and jumping around and it was over. Robin's little butt had bounced from side to side and up and down, but she was still perched atop the tent. We made some adjustments and were back on our way down the trail. We had survived a potentially very dangerous situation. The outing was successful and enjoyable. I think the kids had a good time. For me this began a lifelong love of the area, and, to this day, a continuing desire to return to it. I would do this many times throughout the years. This was a very special place of memories for Liberty and me.

One of many learning experiences occurred about this time. I had decided to take a ride by myself in and around Hudson. I drove down to the feed bunk side of the pasture, parked the car, and caught up Liberty. As the other horses started moving away from the gate, I took Liberty across the barrow pit, tied his lead rope to the door handle of the car, and returned to close the gate. About that time, I heard loud kicks at the car followed by the awful sound of glass breaking. Turning around, I saw Liberty had backed into the car door, panicked at being left by everybody, and responded by kicking the daylights out of my car door! Lesson to be learned...consider carefully how and what to tie a horse to.

I decided I would take my family across the river to see the rocks which had Indian figures on them. We saddled up at the pasture, rode double down to and across the river, and over to the wall markings. After spending some time leading the horses along the wall, we mounted and I turned around and headed down the hill toward the river. I don't remember anything else until I awoke to find myself sitting on the ground, propped up against the horse trailer. Gary told me to sit still while he took care of the horses, then he was taking me to the emergency room in Lander. Another blank until I looked up at someone in white who told me I had had a fall off the horse. Later Gary told me Liberty took off "crow hopping" (jumping) down the hill, I went off with Robin clinging to me (thank heavens she landed on top of me), and apparently I ended up with only a mild concussion.

Commanding respect from but being gentle with his horse family, Liberty continued to be a fierce protector. When another potential intruder came down the fence line, a terrible fight right at the fence resulted in Liberty being caught in barbed wire. I found him there the next day with his leg and knee bones exposed. It was a wonder he still had the lower part attached, and that the bleeding had stopped and crusted over the torn tissue. After a slow and difficult trailer loading for the trip to the vet and an equally difficult unloading, we learned there was a lot of damage done. The tendons had not been severed, only badly damaged. Dried tissue and skin would be removed and treatment would begin. Two weeks of recovering at the veterinarian's clinic would be followed by controlled recuperation at home.

When we were notified that Liberty could go home, we needed to learn how to do the treatments and rewrap his injury. Twice each day his bandage needed to be taken off, dried flesh and scabs removed, the whole area gently washed, ointment applied, and bandages rewrapped. I watched the vet do everything while Liberty was in a squeeze chute and secretly wondered how we were going to get all this done at home. The complete treatment was to be done for a week, followed by once daily for another week, then checked by the vet to ensure healing from the inside out with no infection or "proud flesh" (abnormal tissue growth) present.

Our first attempt to treat Liberty involved me holding the lead rope while Gary worked to remove the bandage. Out came the leg attempting a kick sideways and dancing around. After several tries, we decided it would be up to me. I tied Liberty to a really stout corral post and began to slowly work my hand down his back, down his hip, and almost touched the bandage. The leg came out and up but did not kick. I stopped but kept my hand in contact with him, talking all the while, assuring him quietly that we needed to do this. Several times he turned his head to look, but I continued talking and working at getting the bandage off. Slowly I began the treatment. I could tell it hurt a lot when I worked at removing the scabs and areas oozed bloody liquid. Sometimes he raised the leg but as it went back down I continued. Often we took breaks, and I eventually happily announced I was finished. I was very much aware of the fact that he was showing a greater degree of trust and I knew bonding had taken a gigantic leap. This became more apparent as time went by.

The vet gave us assurance that healing was progressing nicely and soon the bandages were not necessary. Liberty was allowed to come out of the corral and could move around the yard to enjoy bites of grass. Sometimes, if the sprinkler was running, he would move into the spray or even over the sprinkler. How comical he looked if the water stopped because he was standing on the hose. It was now possible to do things with him that I wouldn't have even considered before. Spending more time with him led to my riding bareback a lot and doing goofy things like putting a straw hat on his head for a picture. He even accepted me putting my sheltie/poodle mix dog, "Shelly", on his back. (This turned out to be extremely important in later years. Some of this early "training" also would come in very handy in unusual situations later on. And it began an ongoing mutual trust between Liberty and me.)

Gary and I took another weekend trip to Shoshone Lake. We had to camp in an area that was quite a ways from the creek where we would get our water. Someone else was already in the campsite we had stayed in previously. We needed to figure out a way to carry water. Our containers wouldn't hold much so we used double garbage bags and rode bare back. The water sloshed and ran down the horses backs and legs even though we knotted them as tight as we could. We were pretty soaked, too. A learning experience for the horses and a funny memory for us.

On this same trip, we had followed a creek for a ways and ended up crossing it in a very muddy, boggy area to head back. Gary, on Babe, was in the lead. Apparently Liberty thought he knew an easier route. Stepping onto a large rock half buried in the gumbo muck turned out to be a bad decision on his part and we started to slide backwards. My holding tight to the saddle horn put lots of pressure on the cinch. As Liberty kind of sat on his butt in the mud, the cinch let go and I ended up "riding" the saddle into the muck beside him. Scrambling out of the way (I could barely stand up), I was laughing so hard I just stumbled around. The rest of the trip was uneventful and enjoyable.

Wanting to do more horse packing, we planned a weekend in the Stough Creek Lakes area. The trail head is reached by driving up the dirt and gravel Loop Road out of Sinks Canyon. On that particular day the road was in very bad condition with almost continual washboard ruts and ridges. We hadn't driven very far before I saw a most horrendous sight. Looking out the passenger window into the rear side mirror, I caught sight of the trailer door swinging open and then all four of Babe's feet up in the air. Thankfully, I have not been a believer of tying the lead rope and she had just done a somersault backwards on her back when the door latch bar had popped up letting the door swing open. As soon as Gary got the truck stopped, I ran back to Babe, who was already getting up. She had gravel and dirt and dings all down her back and all over her neck and legs but nothing running blood. I needed to wash her all over so I headed back down the road towards the river with her. Gary got turned around and, amazingly, Babe didn't hesitate when I asked her to get back into the trailer. Down at the river I found a place to lead her into and began washing her all over. After about half an hour, we decided we would load up and drive up to Worthen Reservoir, spend the night, and decide what to do next. The next morning Babe was a little stiff so I rode her around bareback for a few minutes, which helped us decide we could go on with our plans. Gary carried all our gear and I rode without the saddle. The easy pace we rode at got us all in and back out of the Stough Lakes with no other major problems. To this very day, I always tie down the latch bars on the doors of the trailer.

Liberty and I began to spend many hours on short solitary rides up and down town streets, up the road to the dump area, and out on the BLM land which surrounds town. A co-worker at the job I was employed at became a frequent riding companion. His wife was happy to stay home and not be asked to ride because she really was not enjoying the experience at all. Some girl friends were happy to go on short rides with me. A few rode Liberty and some had their own horses. Often we rode on nice winter days. I enjoyed the updates on gossip as much as the rides.

A rather bewildering situation became evident as spring approached. It appeared that Babe had started "making bag". This meant her udder had begun to fill with milk! I had heard of situations where a false pregnancy or sympathy pregnancy had occurred. This didn't seem to be the case. I knew she hadn't been exposed to any other horse, and more importantly, Liberty had been gelded almost two years before. How could this be??? Every day I checked on her and knew she was close to foaling.

Remembering what the vet had told me made me very apprehensive. One morning on my way to work, knowing she was very close, I drove down the road near the feeding area. Babe was slowly circling, followed by efforts to lay down, then circling again. As she turned I could make out two small hooves emerging. Horses have a very short time in labor and need to deliver the colt or one or the other could die. She was in trouble.

Climbing through the fence, I could see she was wet with sweat and breathing hard. "How can I help you, Babe?" As I followed her around in a circle, I reached out and took hold of the little hooves and pulled gently back. She stopped, looked back at me, and down we went to the ground together. She pushed and I pulled and a wet little thing in a gooey bag ended up in my lap! I yanked at the sack until the colt's head was free and then worked at squeezing out any mucous as it began to breath and struggle a bit. Poor Babe. She was totally exhausted. She occasionally raised her head up to make soft sounds and then back down on the ground. I was fighting back tears as I worked on the colt, so afraid for Babe. "Please don't die, girl. This baby needs you. I'll help but it needs you." "Dear God, we need your help, too. Please help Babe." After what seemed eternity, Babe began to get up and try to take care of her baby. I was able to break the umbilical cord and had gotten some tissues from the car to wipe off most of the gooey mess and Babe finished the job. I hugged her neck and kissed her, all the while thanking her for what she had just done. She had almost given her life for this effort.

After helping the colt up and making sure it found the important first drink of nourishment, I paused to look the wobbly creature over. It was a mixture of tan, black, brown, even some white near the little hooves and on its forehead. I was looking at a miniature sized version of Liberty. Even a horse colt at that. Already, in my mind, his name was going to be Sandy. I wondered what the vet and A.Q.H.A. would think and say about this little guy. Although he was rather thin, everything appeared okay. His long legs, neck, and back indicated he might grow taller and bigger than any of the rest of his horse family. This, indeed, proved to be true.

I filled out the registration request for SANDY BOY BARLEO and waited for it to be approved. Instead, I received a list of questions pertaining to the fact that Liberty was gelded. The vet had told me to let him know if there was any problem with registering Sandy. When I showed him the questionnaire, he said to send pictures of Liberty and Sandy and tell them my vet was willing to do blood tests to prove relationship. I did as he said and soon received the approved registration. The apparent explanation for all the questionable circumstances is that there is "one last shot" after gelding that can last a very long time and be effective if the mare is just right and receptive. My Babe and Liberty had achieved this and the result was our "miracle mistake", Sandy. One other fact about all this is that I was not able to have a child due to radical surgery when I was a teen. I look at Sandy and as much as I love my adopted daughter, Robin, I will always be thankful for the unusual events that led to my helping Babe with this "miracle". You, the reader, have probably heard the statement about how God works in mysterious ways...

When Sandy was a few months old, Gary and I wanted to resume our trips to the mountains. We planned to take Babe and

Sandy to the trailhead, I would stay with them, and Gary would return home and bring Liberty. Babe loaded fine, but Sandy wouldn't step up into the trailer. We tried everything but were not able to get him in. Gary decided he would just pick Sandy up and put him in. What resulted was the hide being stripped off both front and back legs. Instead of going to the trailhead, we went to the vet. After cleaning, treating, and wrapping all the areas, the vet suggested we leave Sandy with him and go ahead with our planned trip.

In camp the next morning, we could tell Babe was really full of milk. Would she let us "milk" her and take some of the pressure off? She did and we kept some of the milk and put it in pancake batter. We also tasted some of it. It was thin and a little sweet. I think Babe had less pressure and we had fun doing it.

When we picked up Sandy he was relaxed from the sedative he had been given by the vet. We were able to get everyone home with out any other mishaps. Sandy was hungry and Babe was happy to oblige. The injured areas healed up with no visible scarring. That summer became a time of conflict for Gary and me. We separated often and eventually the decision was made to divorce. Liberty became my confidant. He would stand quietly while I let go of all the pent up emotions I was feeling. Often his neck was wet from my tears. He was such a good listener, just exactly what I needed. At some point I made up my mind to continue riding, camping, and enjoying the outdoors with my horse family. I wasn't going to give up doing that, even if I had to go by myself. I had learned a lot and I had always been independent and self-sufficient. I had friends to ride with and I made a point of talking to anyone about places to go. I had all the equipment necessary and had experience.

My co-worker friend, Tony, and I exchanged bits of information about riding and new places to go. Eventually, we started going on short rides together, sometimes accompanied by Tony's wife, sometimes with a friend or two of Tony's. On one particular ride, three of us were headed up a foothills trail heading into the Wind River Mountains north west of Red Canyon. The further we went, the further behind I was. My Liberty wasn't conditioned as good as the other two horses. I needed to have a "pit stop" and there wasn't much cover to be found on this face, so, a small tree would work.

Getting back on my horse, I looked around and ahead but could not see the others. I continued along the faint trail and began to worry about where they were. Getting more anxious by the minute, I called out several times, ending with "where the H... are you S...o....b's?" No answer came and soon the trail turned to the right towards some big boulders and a few trees. There I found my friends, laughing their heads off. The spot and small tree I stopped at has since had the unofficial name of "p... on it tree".

2

ADVENTURES WITH MISSY

I couldn't always find someone to go with me, especially if it involved a long ride or camping overnight. I was anxious to make another trip to Shoshone Lake. Besides being a beautiful area to visit, I felt very confident about finding my way in and back out. I had been working with Missy and wanted to pony her along with Liberty so she could learn from him and get some experience in the mountains. The preparation went well and I very much enjoyed the thirteen mile trip from the Middle Fork trailhead to the lake. We had some questionable moments when the trail got really faint in a rocky area but Liberty was able to get us back on good trail when I was finished wandering around looking for it. I think he remembered from previous trips when I had just been sight seeing along the way following Babe and Gary!

When I had the horses taken care of and camp set up, I settled into enjoying the area and the experience so far. My little dog, Shelly, alerted me that something was happening by the horses. Missy was stomping around on her picket line and Liberty was wandering down the trail we had come in on. He had pulled his picket stake out of the moist ground it had been stuck into. I took it off so I could replace it in a better place. He took a few bites and began to move again. Missy's wet rope had shredded loose at the leg hobble and she was now moving loose as well. As I nonchalantly tried to walk up to Liberty, off he went with Missy following close behind. Keeping my cool, I followed down the trail, calling them. Surely they would stop and graze in the big meadow not too far away. As I walked out of the trees and surveyed the big meadow, my heart sank. They were nowhere to be seen. The tracks went right back the way we had come in. I sat down on a big rock to think this all through.

A few days before I had left, I had excitedly told my neighbors, Ruth and Gene, about my plans. Gene had jokingly told me he would come "rescue" me if I needed to be. Sitting there on the rock thinking over my options, a noise got my attention. It was a dirt bike rider who was as surprised to see me as I was him. I explained my situation and the fellow said he would be happy to call my friend when he got out of the mountains that evening. I really didn't expect Gene to come but probably one of his grown sons would. They were experienced ranchers and packers. With no other possibilities, I returned to camp with my dog and made an attempt to laugh at my folly. It was a long night.

In the morning, I cleaned and packed up my camp. Having nothing else to do, Shelly and I took up our post on the rock at the edge of the meadow. Dozing in the warmth of the September sun and enjoying the fall colors, I awakened to my dog barking. Coming out of the trees and walking up the trail was an older man in bib coveralls. It was none other than Gene. I hurried to meet him and thank him for keeping his word. Behind him came his son, Ed, and Ed's daughter, each leading extra horses, and bringing up the rear was a friend of Ed's with an extra horse. Gene had ridden part way but chose to walk a good portion of the way. What a guy! What a friend!

After packing my camp and things on a horse, we headed out. On the ride out, they told me my horses had followed the trail all the way to the trailhead and on to the river to drink, passing right by the forest service work station. Some summer workers had spotted them, caught them easily, and put them in the corral by their building. What a relief it was to see them watching us come down the trail.

My enjoyment of riding and exploring new places continued. I cultivated a new source of information. Skip, a backcountry forest service ranger, became a good reference for riding at my level. He gave me encouragement as well as invaluable safety pointers. Soon I was going to places on the map others talked about but never attempted to go to. I was getting more experience and knowledge. And I was learning that Liberty could teach me a lot and sometimes make the best decisions. If I insisted, he would do as I asked, but sometimes he would balk and often I would realize later why he had been right. I learned to respect his actions.

Tony and I often rode with a rancher friend. I got to see more new areas and even though I ate a lot of dust, it was fun to go. We chased and pushed cattle on the desert areas around Hudson, above and around Red Canyon, and on up to summer pastures in the Wind River Mountains. Some times I rode from Hudson to the ranch to spend time and just hang out. I could ride there along the BLM two tracks in about an hour. Occasionally, a herd was pushed up and back into mountain pastures near Canyon Creek, south and west of Cherry Creek, and Snow and Ed Young Basin. There are fantastic views back there, into some really remote areas. Some of the trails and terrain made me thankful I was riding my reliable Liberty.

After getting exposed to country like that, Tony and I would return to explore side trails. His hunting eye was always scouting for good places to find game. As fall approached, we planned some hunting trips. After successes bagging deer, we talked about elk hunting. Tony had gotten a moose tag and that hunting trip was planned.

The area for moose hunting was near Fish Lake, in the Sheridan Creek area west of Dubois. Tony's wife, Tina, and a friend, Jim, that Tony had worked with would also come. To help with the shortage of horses, I would also bring Missy. She was progressing nicely and Tina would do okay with her. Jim assured us he would le to pack any meat on his horses and that he knew how to up game.

The area we would hunt in was frequented by bears so we would need to pack any meat out of the kill area. I brought my packing gear but didn't really anticipate using any of it. Tina rode on our first scouting day. It was pretty strenuous and she decided she would rather be the camp tender. It was great to return to camp at dark and find a yummy meal waiting for us.

The season opened and we were out riding from dawn to dusk. In one area it was decided Jim would ride along a particular trail and Tony and I would circle around to meet up further on. I was alternating horses and that day I was on Missy. As the afternoon advanced, we realized we had been getting too far away from Jim's trail and would need to head up to it. Our faint game trail had been dropping in elevation so we needed to climb up a really steep hill. It turned out to be so steep, the horses clawed their way up through boulders and stands of trees. I was afraid to stop long enough to jump off, and if it wasn't for my arms and hands wrapped around Missy's neck, I would have slid right out of the saddle and down her back.

As we leveled out, we caught sight of moose ears, then much movement, as the animals turned and ran off. At least we now knew some were in our area. The next day we headed back to the area and Tony was able to bag a huge 5 year old bull moose. The guys hemmed and hawed about how to start quartering out the monstrous carcass. I voiced my limited knowledge and between the three of us, we had chunks of meat ready to be loaded on horses. As Jim worked at getting his horses to accept the smelly, bloody pieces, we realized he was not going to be able to pack any meat.

I remembered being told to smear warm blood on a horse's head and even up into their nostrils so that it would be what they were smelling and then they would let the meat be packed on them. I did this with my horses and it worked. Jim never even got to that point. His animals had been babied too much. I had always tried everything so that my horses could not tell what was right and okay or not so. Even when I didn't do things the "correct" way, it was our way so it was okay.

We had the head and cape on Tony's horse and front quarters in my old canvass soft panniers on Missy on my riding saddle. Down the trail we went towards camp. The rest of the carcass had been hoisted up and tied in a tree. Hopefully nothing would find it before we got back for it. Missy trudged down the trail but the load was so heavy on her and it kept sliding forward no matter how tight it seemed. Eventually the worn out canvas gave way and several times the whole affair ended up so high on her neck, she just put her head down and unloaded all of it right off on the ground. No thrashing around, she just dumped it off right where she had stopped. The final solution was to run the back cinch around her butt, which helped hold the load back.

It had been such slow progress down the trail, we had to do all the repacking in the dark. The lights of camp were a wonderful sight. The rest of the carcass was packed out on Liberty and Tony's horse the next day. All of it was okay. A picture and article appeared in the paper, the mounted head and cape hung on Tony's living room wall, and I ate lots of moose meat. I was so proud of my horses, the memories of that hunting trip are still fresh and make me smile. We spent more time hunting for elk in the South Pass area and I got more confident about riding in remote areas by myself. I was so inquisitive about new areas. Where did this trail go to and what did this country look like. At home, I spread out my maps and day dreamed about new places to explore.

To accommodate my increased amount of riding time, I intentionally chose to work at seasonal jobs. I did landscaping and yard work, federal fire fighting, catering, and the like. Jobs were plentiful enough and I learned quickly so I got by financially.

One job I got even allowed Liberty to help me make money doing something I really enjoyed. I was one of several riders hired to bring a herd of cows out of summer mountain pasture to be trucked to their winter feeding area. We met at Louis Lake Lodge on a snowy fall afternoon. The plan was to ride into Maxon Basin early the next morning to begin looking for and rounding up the scattered animals. It was very cold and a nasty fog made it even more uncomfortable. We hadn't ridden far when a few animals appeared, walking toward us. The older animals were used to the routine and were headed out! It wasn't long before we had the whole herd out at the pickup area and loaded up. The four day job planned only lasted one full day but we were paid for the original amount agreed on. We all were pleased.

A day ride that Tony and I did on Red Butte out north of Lander turned into another "misadventure". It started out just fine and we both were enjoying the ride. We came to a barbed wire fence with no gate in sight. Riding along the fence we found a spot where most of the wires were hanging close to the ground. Tony would stand on the wires so I could lead the horses and step over the wires. As I lead Liberty through, he was trying to cross over the lowest point of the wires, which was near Tony. The horse bumped him off balance and knocked Tony off his feet. As he hit the ground, the wires sprang up in between Liberty's legs. Liberty was caught in the wire and ended up falling on Tony's leg. Liberty listened to me and didn't try to get up. Tony was able to get free and out of the way. When we were able to get Liberty out of the wires, I got a look at his hind legs. One had been damaged so bad and had cuts in the same old places. Wrapping a kerchief around the area helped stop the worst of the bleeding and weeks of daily care got Liberty back to where we could ride again.

The winter days were often nice and I enjoyed many rides outside of Hudson. Sometimes friends would ride with me and many times I would pony another of my horses along. This helped in their training. They learned much from Liberty. As the upper country opened up in early summer, I returned to exploring new trails. Many times I tried to find someone to go to Shoshone Lake with me. Tony and I did a day ride that made a big circle of two trails that went to the lake but we didn't go all the way in and ended up coming out in the dark anyway. It was a long ride.

By late summer I planned a trip to Shoshone Lake again. I would ride Liberty and pony Sandy, who was now three. I had been on his back and put a saddle and bridle on him a couple times in the pasture. He didn't know anything but would learn from Liberty's actions. Mountain and trail riding was very different from road walking around Hudson.

I totally enjoyed the ride in. The weather was beautiful and we took our time. How I enjoyed doing this again! When the horses were picketed out and camp was set up it was still early enough to enjoy the late afternoon. That is until I noticed Liberty was not connected to his hobble and was wandering away from camp.

In some way the hobble had opened up and was lying on the ground. I again tried to get ahead of him without spooking him. He figured it out immediately and picked up his pace. As he moved away, I turned back and grabbed a lead rope. Quickly I snapped it on Sandy, praying Liberty would not leave without him. After tying Sandy to a really stout tree, I followed tracks down to and across the big meadow. The horse was nowhere to be seen. Hopefully he would come back when Sandy didn't follow.

Back at camp, Sandy was hollering his head off and trying to get loose. I put the other lead rope on him and tied it to a tree on the other side of him. Cross tying would hold him better, but soon he literally did a flip over and was on his back. As he got back on his feet, I tied his leg hobble to one of the trees and this pretty much held him. He didn't settle down for a long time. Most of the night I sat near him, talking so he would know he wasn't alone. Since his baby days, he had always expressed his closeness to me. I was the first sound and smell he had experienced and we had a special bond. My talking helped calm him and released some of my own frustrations.

Morning came and I hashed over solutions in my mind as I cleaned up my camp. I decided I would saddle up Sandy and hopefully we could make it back out to the trailhead. When we were both ready, I undid all the ropes. After a couple light bounces, I was in the saddle. I asked him with a light heel touch to move. No reaction resulted so I asked him several more times. When he finally reacted, he went straight up and over backwards between the two trees he had been tied to. As we began to go over, I was already getting out of the stirrups and pushing sideways away from him so he wouldn't land on me. Scrambling out of his way, I hung on to the reins. Tears filled my eyes and I let go with a stream of cussing. "You could have killed me! What were you doing? Are you crazy?"

His eyes were huge as he looked at me but he just stood there. I turned and stomped over to and down the trail. He followed along and soon seemed to have quieted down. I stopped to rest and wondered if I wanted to walk out 13 miles. Turning him back up the trail, I again got back up in the saddle. This time a couple steps were followed by a couple more and presently we were making our way down the trail. Occasionally, I would stop him or turn him around to make sure I could control him. A few things along the way looked threatening to him, but stopping, checking them out, and my using words and touches of assurance would calm him down and we would go on. My years of working with my other horses gave me a sense of confidence that seemed to radiate to Sandy and he responded with trust. It was the beginning of his education to become a great trail horse.

Liberty was not at the trailhead and no one had seen or heard of him. Wondering where he could be, I called or went to see everyone I could think of who might know something. No one had any encouraging news. Many people gave me suggestions of others to contact. I followed up on every one. I rode Sandy back up the trails we had been on, calling out Liberty's name, hoping he would hear and answer or even appear. Sandy and I followed other riders who were in the nearby areas. One couple offered to show me the back country along Squaw Creek. That trip proved to be a real challenge physically for Sandy. Some washes we went up were so steep Sandy would have to scramble or find another way to go up. We both learned a lot and he really muscled up.

After two weeks had passed with not one scrap of information, I was really depressed thinking someone else had him or he was dead. One rancher, Reed Allen, who lived in Sinks Canyon, had cattle up above and knew the area well. When I had called him, he said he hadn't seen a buckskin horse but did I know of anyone who was missing a black horse? He had been using binoculars to watch this animal up on Sawmill Point. As there was a bit of grass and a small spring up there, he had decided to just keep watching from his house to see if it would find it's way down. This would be backtracking, as there was no other way off the point. He would wait a few more days before going up to check on it.

A couple days later Reed called and asked, with a chuckle, would I like to come pick up my horse! He had him and he was fine. Reed had gone up, and as soon as he got close enough and the sun was not behind Liberty, he could see it was my dark buckskin boy. Liberty had called to him and went right up to him as he approached and put a lead rope on him. When I pulled up with the trailer, he really got excited and it was a wonderful greeting for both of us. I think he was as glad to see me as I was to see him. His neck was wet with his excitement and my tears of joy. And, there was a happy reunion of all the family' horses shortly after.

I really had never thought about having my horses branded, but after the second run off situation with my horses, it began to make real sense to me to have it done. The areas that I rode were often near Reservation boundaries. I also frequently rode in or near designated Wilderness. If any of my animals were loose and rounded up by an unscrupulous person, chances were strong I might never get it back.

Someone suggested I have my animals sedated by a veterinarian, and branded without negative reactions. This seemed like a good idea and I mentioned it to Tony. He and his friend, Jim, both decided they would also like to have it done for their horses. Arrangements were made to bring all the horses on the same day and pick them up later that day. The brandings turned into a fiasco and over half of them were pretty well botched and difficult to read, even after they were healed over. A couple of the horses were banged up pretty bad, including Tony's. Apparently, the whole thing was not carried out as planned. I've always had negative feelings about the whole regrettable experience. But, at least now, they were all branded and could be positively identified. Soon after, I had lifetime brand inspections on all of them.

3
HIGH COUNTRY

Any time I got into a discussion about horses, the two run off adventures with Liberty would be revisited. Same horse, same location, same time of the year within days. Who would think that could happen? One person that I talked with at length was the man giving me a permanent at the beauty shop that following winter. I told him of my frustration at not always being able to find someone to go with me. I still wanted to go and a lot of the time it meant going by myself. He and some of his fishing buddies had a six day pack trip to Washakie Lake planned for the following summer. I was thrilled when he said I was welcomed to tag along.

They were taking a limited number of pack horses and Jim would let me borrow an oversized set of nylon saddle bags with a compartment for my sleeping bag. I could tie my pup tent on behind that. I could stay only three days because of my work schedule, but, with my knowledge and experience, I should be able to retrace the route back out. I was so excited. Washakie Lake is near the Wind River Reservation boundary and right up on the continental divide.

This would be a new trail head, new country, new trails, great views and challenging terrain. I rode Liberty often that spring and early summer to get him in good condition. Good thing I did because those experienced packers really hoofed along at a fast pace to make the lake by late afternoon. I remember how fantastic the views were and how much affect that pack trip had on me. I loved using the big saddle bags and all the enjoyment I felt further fueled the fires of exploration and adventure.

The guys all went off and did their fishing and such. I walked part way up to the pass and enjoyed relaxing in camp, pouring over my maps to orientate myself and understand the lay of the land. Deep down inside me I could already feel a desire to return to this area and explore more of the trails that seemed to go everywhere. Boy-o-boy, was I hooked or what?

Another "husband" that rode with me was a neighbor, John. He had ridden from Dickinson Park trail head south to Smith Lakes. Due to my work schedule, I was not able to go when he did so I would ride from the Middle Fork trail head and meet him at Smith Lake. I left early but had not estimated the riding time close enough. Darkness overtook me in Sanford Park. I was familiar with that trail but not the part that goes to the lake. It would be best for me to find a suitable place to camp. I decided on a spot where I could bed down in the bowl of a large boulder. An old fire pit showed others had stopped here, too. My dog, Shelly, Liberty, and I would wait for morning to go on.

I woke early to find a visitor. A young doe stood about twenty feet away. She eyed me as I talked softly. My dog didn't bark or growl so she continued browsing. As she slowly moseyed her way into the bushes, I got up and got ready to go on up the trail. Apparently, she had been more inquisitive then afraid. I marveled at how pleasant the experience had been for me.

I took the trail that headed up to Smith Lake and was surprised to run into John coming down it. He was relieved to see me because I had not made it into his camp the previous evening. He said there had been a problem bear bothering campers and the bear was reportedly disposed of recently. This had worried him so much he had kept his fire roaring brightly so I could find his camp in the dark. We rode on up the trail to Dickinson Park where he was parked. I spent the night back down at Shoshone Lake and rode on out the trail to Sinks Canyon the next day. I very much enjoyed the trip, even though it was not what we had planned. At least it had been a positive difference.

John and I rode to several places I was not familiar with. We did a ride to the Cathedral Lake area. I remember we ran into some very hard going so John walked up a trail that disappeared in a jumble of boulders. It was no place to try to go with a horse. We were on the back side of the mountain from the Bears Ears trail which goes into the Washakie Lake area. Many destinations in the mountains are reached by limited trail access. You can't just go cross country or directly across to where you want to be. The terrain can be unbelievably rough. It could be totally impossible to navigate. Some trails are still in place where they were originally used by tribes, explorers, and animals.

My friend at the forest service told me about the short cut trail to get to Deep Creek Lakes. I started out with Liberty and Shelly and the first few miles were uneventful and enjoyable. I had reached a small meadow where Liberty could grab a few bites while I had a snack. As I began to mount up, Liberty danced around and I scolded him. Shelly got concerned and was too close didn't seem to be broken bones but it was very tender and she wouldn't step on it. We had many miles to go and I couldn't see her going the whole way hopping along on three legs.

I managed to coax her up on a tree trunk laying sideways on the ground. Getting Liberty next to it, I reached out and snatched her by the back of her neck and popped her in front of me in the saddle. She squirmed a little, but, soon figured out a comfortable position and up the trail we went. Being a sheltie/poodle mix, she wasn't very big or heavy and balanced herself just fine. Once in a while I would stop and swing her back off on a rock or tree trunk so she and I could both take a short break. Pretty soon all I had to do was point to the place she should get up on and she would climb or jump up there and wait for me to grab her.

Liberty was well aware that she was up on his back and even if she barked or made some other noise, he just pricked his ears and gave little sign of any concern otherwise. The early years of doing unorthodox things was paying off. Many dogs ride on horses but they get trained to ride mostly behind the rider. I was using oversized saddle bags and with my small tent in the middle, there really wasn't room for Shelly. I felt better about her being where I could hang on to her if I needed to.

I took the shortcut trail and we continued along. We were in sight of Deep Creek which would take us to the first lake. I planned to camp there or at the trail intersection with Ice Lakes trail. I had been told about the ease of seeing golden trout (which are more orange in color) from the edge of some of the lakes. On and on we followed the trail up through the trees. It was beginning to seem further than it should be. I didn't want to camp in the trees so a rocky, wet, open area would have to do. I could always ride further the next day. The wind had picked up and darkness was getting closer. There might not be anywhere better for a long way.

I woke to a light but cold rain. The elevation was high enough that I could see a possible snow flurry. I decided it would be wiser to head out and try making it to the lakes another time. Liberty made good time back down the trail. Shelly got a ride most of the way, but she also got good at doing the rock or tree trunk thing. I don't ever remember her getting stepped on again. We did run into some flurries, even though it was summer. Higher elevations can produce solid forms of precipitation at any time of the year.

John was interested in seeing the high, continental divide country so we planned an extended trip which made a big triangle up the middle fork, south across the meadows of Three Forks Park, Gil's Park, Bill's Park, and back north to Ice Lakes and Deep Creek Lakes. I still wanted to make it to the lakes that had the "goldens". We got to the point where the Deep Creek cut-off trail crossed the trail we were on. I told John I wanted to see where I had camped on that previous trip to this area. I rode along the lake edge to where it empties out into a wet, rocky, meadow and as soon I saw the area, I broke into a big laugh. This was where I had camped. I had been within a few hundred yards of the lake but could not see it because I had not gotten up out of the spill way. The comical mystery had been solved! I really enjoyed seeing the "goldens", which actually

ARE orange colored. We didn't fish there but after clambering up on some big boulders, we had a great view of some of the brightly colored fish swimming around.

We continued on our planned triangle route. At one shaded area of the trail was a huge snow drift that extended down a small hill. My Shelly and John's Lily began to scamper around in the snow until John and I decided to have a slide down it, too. We held our dogs on our laps and took turns on the hill. Our horses (tied in the trees) watched while we whooped and hollered. When we resumed our trip down the trail, our clothes were pretty wet but dried quickly. What fun it had been!

The trail drops rapidly near Baer Lakes and as it was twisting through shaded, rocky, places, we cautiously slid our way to the intersection with the Pinto Park trail, which we took to head back out on the third and final leg of our triangle trip. The trails had all been good and easy to follow. The most difficult section was after leaving Pinto Park, where we had to carefully pick our way down through a short but awful bunch of large rocks and boulders. I had been this way before and once again followed the advice given to me by my friend, Skip, at the forest service. We walked and led our horses. Our trip had been great with good weather, nice camp areas, much fun and laughs, fantastic views, and no mishaps. I am always mindful of and thankful for the wives that allowed me to "borrow" their husbands.

Tony and I rode many day rides and also continued to help on round ups. When Tony's horse was laid up for a few days, Tony rode Liberty and got along fine with him. It gave me opportunities to ride my young ones and still have them learn from Liberty. I also did rides on the young horses and led Liberty. I was learning a lot and so were all of them. It got to be a common sight to see me and my "pack train" around Hudson.

In the later years of the 1980's, friends of mine purchased an established greenhouse business in Cody. Because I had experience with gardening, plant propagation, inventory, truck gardening, and the like, Mary asked me if I would be willing to help them open up and run the business. I moved to the property and also found a place for my horses. This opened up a whole new area to ride and explore. Workers for the previous owner stayed on as employees and one of them was as horse crazy and adventurous as I was. Sherry knew something about all the trails on the South Fork and North Fork west of Cody and most points in between. She hadn't been on all of them or very far on others, but she sure was interested in going. Like me, she couldn't always find someone to go with her. Her husband, Gary, was an experienced rider and had his own horse, but he wasn't as "gung ho" as she and I were. Sherry and I rode every drainage west of Cody, all the way to Yellowstone Park's east entrance. I loved every minute of it.

On a ride up the Blackwater drainage, the trail pretty much ended in a huge granite bowl. We tied up our horses in the trees, grabbed our lunches and scrambled up the far side of the rock bowl to eat lunch and enjoy the view. There was absolutely no forage or plants as we neared the highest point we could get to. I absentmindedly played with a good sized piece of wood as I ate, looked around, and wondered how it had gotten clear up there. It finally dawned on me that the wood I was fingering was petrified. Another interesting point along that trail was a memorial site dedicated to a number of firefighters who died fighting a large forest fire many years before.

By late summer, Sherry, Gary, and I had a week long pack trip planned. We would go down the South Fork of the Shoshone, cross over Marston Pass to the head waters of the Yellowstone River, cut across the south east corner of Yellowstone Park, and come out on the Eagle Pass trail to the North Fork of the Shoshone. Wow! We had lots of planning and preparation to do. I would ride Liberty, pack Missy, and Gary would pack Dusty. Sherry wanted to use a pack horse another friend offered her.

The first couple days were pretty much problem free. I did a version of the double diamond pack hitch which tended to loosen up regularly and we spent quite a bit of time readjusting and redoing the packs. None of us really had it down.

As the elevation increased and we followed the trail over rougher terrain, I found myself "holding my breath" more and more. As we went up the trail next to a steep drop into a drainage and a rock face on the other side, I lost sight of my companions around a bend in the trail. A huge overhang of rock was directly above a large rock in the trail. Instead of staying next to the wall, Liberty stepped out around the rock and my heart found itself up in my throat. A wide open view straight down scared me to pieces. Of course, we were okay but my next thought was to scream at Sherry to wait for me to catch up. They were just around the bend waiting for me, so just my eyes said it all. There would be more scary moments on the trip.

We went through a forested area that would be a good campsite and woke up to a driving thunder, lightening, and rain storm. During the time we stayed in our rain camp, Gary and I practiced doing double diamond hitches across Sherry's back as she napped. All of the practice paid off and I was able to do the tie right and we had very little problems with our packs after that.

We crossed a barren slide shale hillside on up to Marston Pass. Sherry had stopped and I called out to her, "why are you stopped? What's wrong?" Her reply was "my horse is looking for the trail." My heart sank as I considered the fact that we couldn't turn around on the very narrow trail that had just disappeared in a slide half way across. We began to move again as each horse picked its way across to where the trail resumed. We got across okay and as I took pictures of the Marston Pass sign and the views surrounding us, I remarked that I was glad we didn't have to go on the awful looking trail in the distance. Gary agreed and Sherry burst out laughing. It was the trail we had just come up! It looked more foreboding from this view than when we had been on it.

At one possible campsite, we had all dismounted and were looking around. A couple of the horses were tied up to trees, including Liberty. Gary's horse could freak out for no apparent reason and it picked that moment to do it. Jumping around, then bucking back down the trail we had just come on, a couple more of the horses started to follow. Sherry ran after her horse and caught it reasonably quickly. Gary shook his head, declaring loudly his horse would probably keep going until it got to where we started from, "just let him go!". I got on Liberty and we hot footed back down the trail. After a couple miles, as I was about to give up following the runaway's hoof prints, Liberty called out. Thinking he was calling his family, it thrilled me to hear a horse answer a short way further. The lead rope on Gary's horse was stuck in a bush that hung out into the trail. He was easy to catch and bring back to our camp site. Gary said his horse wouldn't lead along with another horse, but Liberty had a way of demanding respect. I guess this was what Gary's horse had responded to.

We arrived at an intersection where the map showed we could turn toward Woodard Canyon or continue on our same trail which would join up with the other trail further on. On we went. The trail climbed higher and was rocky and barren. We came to a huge snow bridge over a running creek. We got off our horses and checked it all out, trying to decide if we dared go on the snow bridge. The running water we could hear was really scary. Sherry had dropped the lead rope for her pack horse and had her back to it. We heard steps on the trail and there was her pack horse very calmly, nose down, listening, walking over the snow bridge, stopping on the other side. We grinned at each other, then, one by one, we led each horse safely across.

Our trail then began to drop down through a jumble of downed trees and muck. We thrashed our way through and eventually came to the intersection with the other trail. There we found an old sign indicating the trail we had just come over was closed and abandoned. The Woodard Canyon trail was where we should have been. Where we had been was at the headwaters of the Yellowstone River. Oh, well. Not everyone gets to go all the way up there!

Riding on through the Thoroughfare area was wonderful and we spent a night at Ferry Lake. Rain and fog greeted us the next morning but we packed up and headed out for the Yellowstone boundary. As dogs are not allowed in the back country of the park, a cited violation could get you turned around. We certainly didn't want to do that, so my dog, Shelly, was tucked into the front of my rain slicker and rode there with me on Liberty for the whole day until we crossed back out of the park at the Mountain Creek east boundary. A couple days later we ended our adventuresome and memorable pack trip at the Eagle Creek trail head on the North Fork of the Shoshone near the Yellowstone Park east entrance. What great memories.

Sherry and I did another pack trip. This one was a 3 day ride from Turpin Meadows, over Two Ocean Pass, and out of the wilderness at Pacific Creek trail head near the south entrance to Yellowstone Park. We shuttled one truck and trailer to each end. The route we did proved to be a long but very easy ride. It probably is about the easiest way to get into the "thoroughfare".

Two Ocean Pass is hard to locate unless you see the sign because it is so flat. You hardly know you went over a pass. It gets it's name from the fact that the waters run off to opposite directions east and west. We really enjoyed the scenery and great vistas. The Pacific Creek trail head opened up another whole new area for me to enjoy.

4
WYOMING CENTENNIAL WAGON TRAIN

The year I lived in Cody was filled with work, making new friendships, and exploring new country with my horses. When I returned to Hudson, Liberty and I resumed our trips with Tony and my friends who lived in town. I became a volunteer with the Hudson Vol. Fire Department. This eventually led to being called out on wildland and federal fires not only in Wyoming but also in other states. I was out the whole summer of 1988, and when the fire season was finally over, I decided to go out to Santa Rosa, CA. I stayed with friends until I got settled into a place to live and a decent job.

By late spring, I was missing my daughter, my horses, my home, and Wyoming. Home I came and, again, got into the riding routine. By late fall I had called my boss in California and returned to my job there. That winter I heard about a wagon train trek being organized to commemorate the centennial of Wyoming statehood. I wrote for information and, full of excitement, called Sherry.

Sherry had also heard about the wagon train. It was open to drivers, riders, packers, walkers. Emphasis was to be on pioneer period dress and way of life and travel. Participants could join up for an hour, a day, a weekend, or for the serious minded, the whole 30 days. The group would leave Casper the first week of June and arrive in Cody in time for a blowout 4th of July celebration. The 260 mile trek would pass through many towns and communities as it followed the obscure Jim Bridger trail. Many of them planned local celebrations.

I intended to have all of my horse family involved. Sherry would use Sandy as her pack horse and I would alternate with Liberty, Dusty, and Missy, changing off riding, packing, and ponying. I had made arrangements with the committee to have hay provided and all my fees were paid. I was so excited I could hardly stand it.

Days leading up to my return to Wyoming were filled with making decisions, lists, and plans. My California boss gave me total support to decide when to leave. Making plans for complying with the suggested clothing, I began going to yard sales to find blue denim shirts, neck scarves, and the like. At one sale I found quite a few items and told the woman in charge I was also looking for a "used" western type hat. She said her husband had one he used for black powder gun competitions, but she hurriedly told me she was sure it was not for sale. I asked to see it and her husband brought out a great looking black cowboy hat, laughingly telling me he wouldn't sell it. We talked for a bit and after hearing about my plans for the upcoming events, he said he would be very happy for his hat to be part of Wyoming's 100 year birthday celebration. I left with an armful of things and a smile on my face. The fun had already begun!

The day before the start of the event, Sherry, Gary, and I met in the town of Shoshoni. We transferred horses from my 2 horse trailer to their 4 horse trailer and they went on to Casper. I returned home to get my other two horses and hauled them and my tack to Casper.

The first morning was total chaos. Somewhere around 1000 participants and their animals were attempting to get ready to go and everywhere there was noise, confusion, and milling around.

Some animals had never been in a situation like this, much less their owners. There were some accidents right off the bat and some people never even got started. The "circles" (color coded group you were assigned to) were forming up and the line began to move out of the Fort Casper grounds and head down the street. Our green circle was scheduled last and by the time we headed out, the beginning of the wagon train was well out on the route. The line literally stretched for miles on the city streets, which caused gaps to form, then a rush to catch up, and often I held my breath as we trotted briskly around corners. We worked to keep our animals under control and some were not successful. The route was lined by cheering people, traffic routed down adjoining street lanes, honking horns, and every manner of imagined horse eating monster. What a scary yet exhilarating experience!

One wagon and team (out of control) ran into another and another veered into the spectators. During the first couple weeks, it was common to see a helicopter responding to some accident. A number of people didn't stay in their saddle or on their wagon very long. Many came with no experience for the situations they found themselves in. Often Sherry and I rode off to the side to stay out of those kinds of potentially dangerous situations. We and our animals learned a lot. Every day was a combination of good and bad and everything in between. After a bad experience, it was easy to wonder what the heck I was doing. When things went good, I was so happy and thankful to be part of the historic adventure. What an emotional roller coaster this was turning out to be.

Camp sites were another changing situation. New area, new campers, new problems, new activities. Sometimes the rules changed. No vehicles, unlimited vehicles. Hay delivered to you, find your own transport for hay, sometimes no information about the hay. In one situation, green circle was the furthest point from the hay truck. No vehicles could enter the camping areas. No one came around to ask if I had hay coming. Even though I had never pulled anything with Liberty, he was okay with ropes so out came my picket ropes and we rode over to the hay. After some fits and starts, we were dragging our 2 bales of hay along behind to our camp. Good ole Liberty to the rescue. New task mastered.

Sherry had to return home after a week but she assured me she was coming back. When she did, she brought her boy and they rode for a day. She couldn't stay with the wagon train but agreed to meet me at key locations with vehicle access where she could bring me new supplies. I would miss her but I was enjoying some new friendships with others committed to doing the whole 30 days.

Changing terrain became an interesting diversion to slow passage of time. Changing weather also gained importance. Long stretches of dry, hot, and dusty trail conditions could suddenly change to high wind, cold temperatures, and rain. I was prepared for it all but sometimes it was hard to endure, especially when we had reached the camp area and were trying to unpack and set up our camp. Several times the tack ended up in a pile and snacks were dinner until conditions and energy levels improved. A beer and a saddle for a back rest helped speed up the process. I became an expert at tapping down the pressure of a packed can of beer.

Some scheduled distances between camps were short and others much longer. Scenery varied from open prairie to canyons and riparian lushness. We traveled through small communities and several camps were in populated areas. Often vehicle access was very limited or even almost nonexistent. A few caterers were present and prepared food or limited supplies were occasionally available for purchase.

The town of Burlington was almost by-passed but a short stop was quickly scheduled when it was learned that residents expected us and a program was planned to welcome us. The train snaked back and forth, up and down the few streets, in the small community and festivities began. The local "quick stop" sold out of ice cream and other goodies and a long line of riders went through the drive-up window of the "watering hole". I laughed till I hurt as I paid for my cold beer from my horse's back. It was the best beer on the whole trip.

In the beautiful, colored, steep hills of Painted Canyon, a new procedure was performed that echoed of years gone by. Some of the hills were so steep that many of the wagon drivers had to lock their back wheels with logs and out riders were used to hold back front teams. Sometimes experienced wranglers tied ropes to the rear of a wagon and used holding pressure of their ridden animals to slow down the descent. All of this was fascinating to watch by the many people who spread out on the side hills.

As some of the wagons started up the next hill, there were some wagon drivers that were leery of trying to go up, afraid of having their teams balk and end up in a wreck. The driver of an especially large and heavy rig gratefully accepted an offer to switch teams with another driver that had big, strong horses. Some outriders used ropes to help with the pull up the steeper hills.

One memorable incident involved a wagon pulling another wagon. The driver had gotten part way up a long, steep hill when the rear wagon suddenly detached from the front wagon and began to roll back down the hill towards others waiting to begin. Thankfully, the dragging hitch caused the front wheels to turn enough to make the wagon run off the side of the road to a stop.

Drivers and riders were instructed to wait until an incline was clear before starting up but some used gained momentum to get a running start. Liberty and my string got run off the road or trail several times over the 30 days. My horses in turn were pretty apprehensive about rigs or groups coming too close behind us (they never were bothered that way before but were now). Running horses flying by was sometimes a problem. I was aware of several upsets caused by those behaviors. I lost my temper several times. Some knew better and some were innocently ignorant. As a whole, most people did the best they could.

I worked at enjoying the positive aspects of each day. One comical situation for me was when I dismounted behind a bunch of rocks to answer nature's call. As I squatted, one by one, each of my 3 animals spread out their legs and we all peed in unison. I'd say that's a bond.

When we neared the towns of Lysite and Lost Cabin, it was necessary to cross the railroad tracks. Large pieces of wood and plywood were laid across the tracks. Some animals had more trouble getting across than others. Mine looked it over and continued across. I stopped at a fence line and got off to check my packs. A few minutes later, standing between Liberty and Missy, holding their reins and lead rope, all 3 horses started to fidget and try to move forward. Missy's pannier was up against my back as I worked to hold them. As all 3 of them surged forward at once, I heard and understood. They had felt the vibrations and heard the approaching train! As they had never been exposed to a train, there was no way I could hold them. I would end up being drug after the pannier pushed me over. Bending low I reluctantly let go.

Liberty and Missy galloped down the fence line with Dusty hooked to the pack saddle by his lead rope. He eventually pulled hard enough to make the emergency break away string let go. Someone caught him up and tied him to a fence post. Liberty stopped soon after. Missy kept going, totally freaked out. A big Cadillac came by and the driver hollered an offer of a ride to catch up to her. It turned out the driver was an off duty sheriff's deputy and I forgot to thank him in my haste. Unattended animals were a common sight so it was just my folly.

Our camp near Thermopolis was reached early and the word spread rapidly that some school buses were coming to take us into town for some R and R. Many of us enjoyed the town's barbecue and a swim in one of the mineral hot springs pools before returning to camp later that evening. My stinky body rejoiced.

Our entrance into Worland for a rest day was far different. The day before, we had gotten rained on heavily and the wagon train had not moved. My whole affair was wet and it was cold, rainy, and miserable to pack up my camp and put it all on my shivering horses. One of the head wranglers rode by whistling "just walking in the rain" which improved my mood. Sherry was going to meet me in Worland and I was definitely looking forward to that.

The rain stopped as we headed for town. We were allowed to use the rodeo grounds stalls; first come, first served. All three of my horses were in one stall and did just fine. I walked back to the picnic area and sat at a table, tired to the bone. Sherry walked up behind me and tapped my shoulder. I was really relieved to see her. After a shower at the school and a hot meal, I perked up. She had brought new provisions and my horses enjoyed the day off. Things were back on the positive side.

Many activities were going on during the time we spent in Worland. There was a carnival and lots of local booths. Sherry had left so I spent time wandering around looking at things and visiting. There were people I had seen but I hadn't had an opportunity to get acquainted with yet. A man and his teenage son were having a picnic and we got into a conversation about the cheese they were eating. The wrapper said Wisconsin on it. I had been born and spent my childhood there. Gordie had spent time in the state and his boy lived there with his mother. The boy had flown out to be on the wagon train with Gordie. We became a threesome and often did things together. Gordie had a video camera and would ride ahead to film something and his boy rode with me a lot.

One day Gordie came racing back to us, all excited about something going on ahead. We hurried along and saw a big old wooden bridge that crossed a good sized creek. It was high above the water and many animals were balking about going on it. The bank edges were steep and not an alternative for the bridge crossing. As we got near, we saw a 4 up team in a terrible mess on the bridge. The front team of horses had spooked and tried to turn around. As the back team was in the way, the front team was forced off the left side of the bridge. There were no rails and the left front horse was dangling above the water by it's harness, which was pulling the other front horse closer and closer to the edge. What an awful sight.

People were running everywhere, grabbing the horses' lead ropes and trying to hold them while others were cutting the suspended horse out of its harness. Amazingly, the animals were not seriously injured. But there were some freaked out people who couldn't believe what had just happened. We found out later that as Gordie was filming wagons going over the bridge, he had actually got it all on his camera. What a thing to happen! Imagine how often things like it had taken place years ago during the pioneer migrations! As I crossed with my horses, I noticed them eyeing the bridge warily. Training and experience are necessary and valuable.

Gordie and I became good friends and spent lots of time together. Time passed and the adventure was nearing it's end. We had good and bad times, none of which I would change. The 30 days of the trek ended in Cody with a parade to the rodeo grounds and a wealth of memories. Of the thousands of people who had been involved, about 160 had gone the whole way.

Gordie's son returned to Wisconsin and Gordie's planned participation in an Idaho wagon train was not for a couple of weeks. He wanted to see some of the country around Wyoming. Mountains were not new to Gordie but he had never seen mountains like these. While camping near the east border of Yellowstone, we decided on a trip up the trails of Pahaska and Red Creek to a very remote entrance into the park. After crossing the signed boundary, we topped over a hill and headed for the campsite we had reserved at the head of the Lamar Valley. Expecting to see lots of wildlife along the way, I was somewhat disappointed to find our numbered campsite full of holes that bears had dug to find buried garbage from previous campers. I really didn't want to see that kind of wildlife, especially right in our camp area.

We moved on to a different location and still saw no one else and no wildlife. It was a very remote camp. On the way back out, Gordie was merrily trotting down the trail in the lead. That is, until the trail petered out to nothing. Turning around, Liberty picked up his pace and presently he veered off the trail to the right. I asked him to get us back on the right trail. Where he turned off I couldn't see anything that looked like a trail, but topping over a small hill and dropping down, there it was. He found the way back out with no trouble. What great instincts.

I took my horses and things home and Gordie went to Idaho for another wagon train. He wrote several times and then, one day he showed up in my driveway. After a couple days rest for his horses, he was ready to ride and see more of Wyoming. We had taken a car trip through Yellowstone and now he wanted to see more of the wilderness area. I figured out a triangle trip from Dickinson Park back to Graves Lake near the Continental Divide, south down past the Cirque of Towers and Lizard Head Peak, across the Middle Fork trail, and return up through Sanford Park to Dickinson Park. The scenery along the way is beyond words. A properly conditioned and experienced horse is necessary. The time, expense, and work is well worth it.

The trip is vivid in my memory because I had hauled our two horses in my trailer with my Dodge maxi van. The road to the forest campground is steep with two sets of switchbacks. Going back down in my lowest gear on an automatic transmission, my brakes heated up and eventually failed. A potentially terrible accident was averted when I steered into the soft bar pit and turned my wheels uphill, coming to an abrupt stop. The horses were bounced around quite a bit and were happy to get out of the trailer, even though they had a big drop down to the ground. I had held my cool until we were stopped, then totally lost it in a flood of tears and relief. We were all okay.

5
WORK & PLAY

Gordie returned home to Missouri and I returned to riding with local friends. I needed to find some work and a friend I had coffee with regularly suggested I call an outfitter who might have something I could do. I called and explained my situation and what I had in mind. A few days later I got a call to show up at their ranch at a certain time if I was still interested. That first day turned into four seasons of varying types of work with domestic as well as international guests. I did every type of work including camp set up, cooking, transportation, wrangling, horse breaking and training, packing, and guiding. Eventually I was taking my own horse and could ride either with the groups or by myself, as long as my work was done.

The main areas we had trips in were on the Oregon Trail on South Pass, the Middle Fork out of Lander, and the trails northwest of Dubois. I was enjoying some fantastic country with Liberty and eventually, Sandy. More memories. Great Divide Tours and Ray Focht opened up another whole world of riding to explore and enjoy. I am so grateful for all of it.

About this time I started hearing about a group that sounded interesting. It was Wind River Back Country Horsemen. The group met monthly and did trail riding, trail work, education clinics, and other fun activities. Joining the group opened more doors for learning new skills and meeting like minded animal and outdoor lovers. Even though I was not at all interested in holding an office, I participated in every activity there was. When we built corrals at the Worthen Reservoir parking area, I stayed over night and rode Liberty the next day. He was the first to use one of the new corrals. This became a favorite trail head for us.

Another work project the group got involved with was to plank the big black metal bridge on the Rails to Trails river crossing north of Riverton. Many trail user groups joined together to cover the railroad bridge with wood planks so it was useable by all types of travelers including four legged varieties. Even a group of inmates from the nearby prison honor farm helped pound spikes. As I had brought Liberty on the day we finished up the flooring, I again gave him the honor of the first crossing over. He was hesitant at first but we got across and later, back. I was pretty certain none of my other horses would have responded with as much trust as he had, especially since the side rails were not up on it yet. The bridge experience was a good prelude to some crossings I would do in years to come.

The group also occasionally did some arena activities. We set up obstacle courses of small jumps, wooden bridges, plastic simulated water tarps, and the like. It was all for fun with your animal. One competitive packing activity involved using three animals and two people. It started with the bell telling you to get out of your sleeping bag, put on your boots, catch your animals, saddle up and pack two, mount up and ride across a finish line. I asked Tony to come and be my team member. He was game and we had a blast, I laughed through the whole thing.

The last of the goofy things we had in our pile of things to pack was an inflated inner tube. With no apparent way to attach it, I told Tony to put it over Missy's head and hang it around her neck. He did, she let him, I cracked up laughing, and the spectators loved it, too. I think we came in 3rd of 4 places. I always enjoyed those activities. Liberty and the others got used to doing just about anything. And the others just went along with Liberty if they weren't sure.

6

WHATCHA GOT?...ON YOUR HORSE

After my Bears Ears Trail trip to Washakie Lake, I became an advocate of traveling light, using my newly learned technique each time I did a 3-5 day trip. I refined and incorporated new ideas and I discarded what didn't work. Soon I had a well defined system which I began promoting to others.

Some who listened to me thought I was "nuts." Others were convinced I would hurt my horse's back or kidneys. The key to success was to slowly introduce the animal to the added weight and items—just like any packing technique. Time spent "doing" resulted in a working system I began to promote as "horse packing with no pack horse."

When I was available to help with a packing clinic, I got in the habit of demonstrating how I would do up to three days of riding and do quite comfortably with my oversized soft saddle bags. I made up a list of suggestions for what to take, and how to pack enough for the three days. I enjoyed talking with anyone who was interested in how I did it regularly without hurting my horse. Liberty was a patient demonstrator as I handed out my information sheet.

When our group did demos and had a booth at the Game and Fish Expo in Casper, Liberty and I were there. A drawing was held for an outfitter's horseback fishing trip and a teenage girl won. When she realized she had won, she was kind of apprehensive. She said she hadn't been around a horse since she was a little girl and wondered if she could have a short walk around on a horse to refresh her memories. Liberty was recruited. We did a crash course in being around a horse, basic tacking up, and then she did a little ride around the outdoor booths area. She was thrilled and looked forward to her trip. I was so proud of Liberty and how he behaved with her.

Article taken from *Back Country Horsemen of America* Newsletter
Whatcha got?...in the pack box
by Deborah Pierce
Montana BCH
Flathead Club

Handy food items for backpack trip can be found at your local food store at different prices.

Applesauce, in lunch tubs, comes in 100% fruit by the six pack and averages 25 cents per tub—add to **oatmeal, hot cereal or alone with meals , Fruit leather** as 100% fruit and 20 cents each in many flavors. By careful reading, there are "no added sugars"—save those calories for something that counts, like M&M's.

A small can of pork and beans or spaghetti, is an acceptable lunch item for some in place of a sandwich, as is a **can of fruit** and two spoons of peanut butter. There is no rule in the book that one has to have bread and lunch meat.

Costco, just to mention one food outlet, has **individually wrapped cookies** by the case. They stay fresh and travel better than loose cookies. They also have fat-free **Newtons, cornnuts, no fat granola bars**, 100 percent **juice cartons** and a big selection of **sweets and nuts in small packages.**

Eye those containers of syrup, sugar, flour, coffee and mustard. How much will you need for just three days or five? Are you traveling everyday, or having a stationary camp and hanging food? Whenever possible, **reduce amounts into smaller containers**. Mustard squeeze bottles with tight lids work well. Even jelly will squirt nicely from one of these (but not jam).

Good morning! One big pot of boiling water can make **quick oats** and fruit, add your own nonfat powder milk and huckleberries. Make them by the bowl. **Tea or coffee bags,** decaf or full lead. **Hot chocolate**, cream of wheat, grits, 7-grain, etc. You'll have a quick **cleanup with the remaining hot water,** and you'll be slapping leather before sunrise.

Pre-cook bacon before a trip. Yuck—wouldn't that have been a mess in camp and a bear and insect attractant. There will still be enough fat to grease the pan when it is reheated. Bacon bits left? Toss in with **instant mashed potatoes**, on the baked beans, or on the veggies.

Jim Guppy serves a dandy breakfast at hunting camp. Toast bread or sourdough **English muffins** in a dry pan. In a separate skillet **scramble eggs**, bacon bits and pepper or tabasco. Heap on bread, add a slice of **cheese** (make mine no fat please) cover with bread and consume. **One pan and one turner to cleanup**.

I select items based on their lower calories, salt, fat, or sugar content whenever possible. Most packaged items are extrememly high in salt and sugar. **Weight** of items vs. taste and general overall nutrition is always a consideration. **Most important is who's in the wilderness to cook, or hang their food in trees?**

Shelf life is a concern with summer heat. For longer trips, think ahead and plan to eat fresh first, packaged last. **Cabbage, carrots, onions, potatoes and apples store and pack well as does celery, cauliflower, and broccoli.** Chop up a relish selection and enjoy.

The following is my list of suggestions to add to the article written by Ms. Pierce in the BCH Newsletter.

Flash light, candle.
first aid kit,
water filter, bug spray, tool or/and repair kit. matches.
Changes of clothing.
Personal articles.
maps, Canteen.,
Picket line, stake or Hobbles.
Rain gear.
sterno or other light weight cook stove.

CAMERA

Compact, Light weight tent + fly.
Light weight, compressible sleeping bag.
Camp shoes.
Over sized bags with sleeping bag compartment and pommel (horn) bags available at commecial sporting goods, animal outlets. Various sizes + prices.

Horse Packing with NO Pack Horse

Advantages:

Less stock used - Low Impact on Land. Fewer stock to care for.

Fewer packing items - ie, no pack saddle, lash rope, pack cover, etc.

Quick camp duties - No hanging of panniards, Less clean up. Easy and quick food prep.

You can "pack" into the mountains with only your riding horse and minimal equipment.

Disadvantages:

No room for "Kitchen Sink" - large cooking utensils camp chairs, heaters, etc.

Limited selection of Foods, degree of cooking required.

Fewer clothing articles.

Time out on trail, distances traveled limited, camp selection for animal feed important*

Suggestions: repackage food items, use saddle pads under sleeping bag, hang bags using picket rope, do "double duty" on utensils.

Nationally recognised by land agencies, "Leave-no-Trace" advocates. BCH of California, CDTA Vail Conference.

Can be successfully adapted to include 1-5 days, and with timely conditioning of your animal, up to 20-25 miles per day.

Continue going and revising to improve your system! ☺

7
BEAUTIFUL TRAVELS/ TRYING TIMES

A memorable ride I did by myself was for a couple days back to Lonesome Lake on the Divide. I camped along the way as there was nothing at the lake itself. The scenery along the route is absolutely gorgeous. On my way out, I arrived at Pinto Park and decided I would stop on the wide open face and enjoy the view before resuming my ride out. I whipped out my Sterno cooker and heated up a metal cup of hot water and had hot instant coffee and a snack while I absorbed as much of the grandeur as possible. The wide open vistas are inviting teasers that suggest more awaits your appreciation. Indeed, the first peaks to the north are the beginning of the Cirque of Towers. "It doesn't get much better".

My friend, Carol, and I did a fun ride with a group along the highway between Cody and Pahaska Lodge near the Yellowstone Park east entrance. The trip was scheduled for three days but I only had two days off, so we did the first two. The group then continued on along to the park boundary the third day. That part was the most scenic, but we enjoyed what we had done. It was early in June, and Liberty and Sandy were as full of spit and vinegar as any of the other horses.

The BCH group scheduled a ride into an area called Beauty Park. The trail began from the highway, just west of Togwotee Pass, and headed south. Again, because of my work schedule, I had to ride in by myself. The trail was easy to follow and soon we reached the camp area. I was using my big saddle bags and had everything I needed for three days on my Liberty. As we entered the clearing, I heard several calls of greeting and a few of them voiced surprise to see me and my single horse. I think they were worried they would have to "take care" of me for the weekend. This was not so and I did just fine on my own. I was happy for the fun and camaraderie that we shared that weekend. The experience reinforced my confidence level a lot.

Another ride that Carol and I did was potentially dangerous as we were coming down the trail that switches across and down Fairfield hill above Sinks Canyon. We had been up the middle fork trail above the falls for a day ride, and we had turned around and headed back as we saw an approaching thunder storm coming from the west. The dark clouds soon overtook us and lightening crashed behind us. The wind was blowing and I urged Carol to hurry along on Liberty. As we hot footed across the open hillside, a big crash and a bright lightning flash stopped both horses. They both whirled and turned sideways on the narrow trail, not knowing where to go or what to do. It scared all four of us. I actually felt the "hair on the back of my neck move" so I knew it had been very close. I screamed at Carol to kick Liberty in the ass and hang on. We flew down the trail. That's one of the scariest memories I have with my horses. I'm sure Carol has a vivid memory of it, too.

My cousin, Gary who lived in Wisconsin, and his friend, Jim, were interested in hunting big game in Wyoming. They wondered if I could help them set up a seven to ten day guided trip. I told them I would check things out and get back to them. I made the rounds of the agency offices and got as much information as possible. After many phone calls back and forth, they put in for their out-of-state licenses. In the mean time, we both started making plans and arrangements. I could outfit and guide them in the wilderness. They would pay the expenses and I would make the arrangements for using all four of my horses. Among the three of us, we had what we needed for our camp. I scouted the Dunior trails and drainages for a suitable camp site and looked for game sign and trails. When they arrived in late September, we finished our preparations and drove off in excited anticipation.

Opening day came and went with only a couple very distant sightings. Some shooting could be heard and a few of the many hunters were successful. We hunted hard from early morning to dark. A foot of new snow should have improved our odds but soon it was the end of our week and we hadn't fired one shot. We packed up our camp and headed out for the trailhead. Snow, mud, and shaded, icey trail made the going treacherous. The horses all knew we were heading out and they didn't need any encouragement. As Gary, in the lead on Liberty, rounded a switchback, they slid off balance. Down they both went. Gary scrambled out of the way and Liberty got back up. I shouted to Gary to grab Liberty, who was already starting to walk on. Shaken to the core, Gary hollered back that I should care more about him then the horse. I hollered that he had better catch his horse or he would be walking the rest of the way to the trailhead. I knew Liberty was capable of leaving in a hurry!

At the vehicles we visited with an outfitter, Tim, we had met while packing up to go in on our hunting trip. As we told him about our disappointing week, he remarked about how great it was that I had been able to set up and complete the hunt. He felt bad that we hadn't been successful and wondered if we would be interested in spending a day or two hunting in an area that had resident herds but was controlled access by private property. He could give us permission to go in. After details were worked out, we left to go to the new hunting area.

It was early enough yet that we could unload the horses, grab snacks, and ride part way up the side of the mountain. We tied up the horses in the trees and decided to walk at three levels part way around the mountain. I would go up and on the highest level, hopefully to move something into their view. It was several hours before dark and we would all return by then. I walked and walked and walked. Rocky areas prevented me from dropping back down through the trees. The wind came up and it began to snow. I needed to get lower but the rocks blocked any easy route. I began to lower myself down through ledges and giant boulders to try to go back. I surveyed a long drop to a ledge below that appeared to be not far above the trees. Hanging onto a sagebrush, I dropped down and let go. Wrong decision. I was now on a ledge that dropped away in all directions. I couldn't go up, down, or sideways. I was stuck on a rock! Someone would have to come find me.

I spent the night curled up into a ball against the rock wall and did all the things I could think of to stay warm enough. Limited flexing of muscles from toes to head, warm clothing, snacks, and prayers helped me get through a night of howling wind and snow flurries. I actually fell asleep two different times. As I woke up to again realize the predicament I was in, tears flowed. Tears of thankfulness that I woke and then tears of fear of possible outcomes. I burned up the lines of communication with the big guy upstairs.

In the mean time, Gary and Jim had gotten Tim to help them. The horses were kept where they were tied in hopes that I would call out and be heard by them. They would have answered me. Search and Rescue people were brought in but they didn't hear me and I didn't hear them. The night finally turned into another day and I was weighing my options. As the day progressed, we all were pretty worried.

Tim and Gary had decided to return to the ranch and as he turned to head back, Tim heard something and began to yell louder. The wind had carried our voices and I answered him. It took quite awhile for them to find me and get to me but eventually the two found a happy, tearful, blubbering woman. After a very difficult drop from the ledge, my rescuers helped me back to their truck and to a warm shower and nap at the ranch. I was okay physically and mentally, and very thankful. The hunt had not resulted in filled tags but we had all had quite an adventure. Tim will always be my "hero" as I stated in the ranch's guest book.

A difficult experience happened when the BLM asked for some volunteers to transport square, heavy wire panels down a steep hillside to the riparian areas in a canyon along the Sweetwater River. I volunteered with Liberty and Sandy. When I called the other possibly interested persons, everyone either had lost interest in helping or wasn't available. I was on my own. I would do what I could. As the panels were very heavy and bulky to lift up and attach to the pack saddle by myself, it took me a long time to load them on Sandy.

Down the narrow, twisting, trail we walked. Sandy was close to Liberty and eventually he tried to step down off the trail and around Liberty. This caused the weight to pull him downhill. I hung on to his lead rope and Liberty was able to stay on the trail until we got to a more level spot. I decided I was in over my head on this project and I had better quit before I hurt myself or my horses. Unloading the panels on the side of the trail was even worse then loading up. Reporting my lack of success to the BLM was embarrassing but at least we hadn't had a wreck or injuries. We had tried our best.

When Liberty was 20 years old, the BCH group did a pleasure ride that we attended. One of the fellow riders had brought his preteen son along and the horse he was riding was a bit of a handful to control. As we walked along visiting, the boy rode off and began to trot along parallel with us. Liberty turned and began to follow along behind his horse. Our trot increased in speed and soon we were in a lope. Liberty followed the other horse and up and down small hills we went. As we went along on a faint trail, the terrain leveled out and both horses were in a moderate speed gallop. The boy's horse seemed to be under control and the wind flying through my hair was exhilarating. On and on we went. Liberty was enjoying the run, too, and I wasn't encouraging him at all. The boy turned his head and I saw a huge smile on his face. As we began slowing, the air was filled with his laughter and happiness. We turned and headed back towards his dad and the others. Later his dad quietly told me he hadn't been worried a bit because Carole was with his boy. I explained that I hadn't turned Liberty to follow; it had been Liberty that went with him. I had just been aboard for the ride. What a warm feeling I get with that memory.

The BCH group scheduled a weekend get together at Dickey Springs near Oregon Buttes on South Pass, but I was working until 2 p.m. both days. I took Liberty up on Friday afternoon and got in a short ride. Spending the night up there was fun and my camp

We both saw the bear moving through the trees at the same time. Our stopping abruptly caught the bear's attention but he continued toward the trail and crossed it about 20 feet ahead of us. I was talking quickly but quietly to Liberty. We stood in place until the bear had reached the trees on the other side of the trail. There he turned, put his front paws up on a big tree trunk, and looked right at us. As he was almost even with us, I urged Liberty slowly forward, whispering to him, the bear and even myself. If the bear charged, I was ready to hang on tightly to the potential rocket ship I was aboard. Trying not to leave too quickly, I was keeping my side vision on the bear but he didn't move. My heart could stop pounding so hard then.

We had caught up with the bear as he was making his way down the mountainside and he had crossed the trail numerous times because of the switchbacks. That was the reason Liberty had acted the way he had as we turned back on each switchback. We reached the bottom with no more problems. Even though I knew the differences between black and grizzly bears, all I knew was that it had been a BEAR. It had been closer than I cared for but at least it had turned out to be the right way to experience a bear encounter. I had a new appreciation for my Liberty.

On another visit to the Dickinson Park corrals and trailheads, I had given Liberty some hay in a corral after we returned from a day ride. From my maxi van I could hear a commotion in the corral. Looking out the open door, I saw Liberty moving back and forth along my side of his pole enclosure. On the far side, a bear was casually walking along the outside of the corral, stopping to smell the ground, then moving on. A ranger I had visited with earlier that day had told me about a bear that visited the corrals nightly looking for grain left on the ground or scraps from a careless camper. The bear had never caused anyone problems but it was necessary to keep a clean area and be watchful. As it was dark out, I couldn't tell what kind of bear it was, and the ranger hadn't said. It didn't matter, we just needed to be careful.

Dickinson Park has several trailheads and I rode to many different locations. It continues to be a favorite memory maker for me, though it has been quite a few years since I have been there. I did many day rides, overnighters, and three day loops. Most of my visits were by me, my horse, and my dog. Occasionally, I rode with someone else or met up with someone at another location reached by riding from Dickinson Park. Such a beautiful area demands more than one visit to be fully appreciated.

I enjoyed many day rides on Liberty. We frequently camped overnight at the Worthen Reservoir trail head and rode the trail down to Sheep Bridge on the Middle Fork. At other times I enjoyed going over the mountain and down to a long meadow called Bills Park. If I had gotten an early enough start, I turned south and continued on along the river, and one time I hustled along and went on up the steep trail that goes over Sweetwater Gap. Shelly, my little dog, and I went far enough that we were looking out over the desert area but the terrain was not open enough to know what we were seeing. I know it was pretty high as there was a lot of water and mud in the trail as we got to the highest point on the trail. Snow still blanketed the side hills. We kind of clawed our way up and slid our way down. Liberty was happy to turn around and head back.

Carol, my Hudson riding buddy, and I rode to Stough Creek Lakes and she filled me in on how much easier going it was than when she and her husband, Bob, had gone on the old trail. The newly rebuilt route was a definite improvement over the trail of previous years. It was another of the routes I did frequently. Sometimes I would stop for lunch at the first lake and a few times I rode further up the trail. At a distance further up, the going gets too rough for a horse and the upper lakes are accessible only by foot.

I also enjoyed riding out of Grannier Meadows. I had been told about the Sioux Pass Trail and that it was an easy, short distance to ride. I rode along for awhile and after a gradual climb, the trail seemed to be slowly dropping as it became a tunnel through the trees. Down, down, down it continued and I decided I needed to turn around. Had I missed a turn off along the way? The next time I visited the Forest Service office, I asked Skip about whether I had gone on the right trail. He laughed as he asked me if I remembered passing some very stout posts on my left. I did remember because that was where the trail seemed to begin dropping as it entered the trees. The posts were for the Sioux Pass sign which is taken down in the fall. THAT point was the pass. It was so gradual

I hadn't realized it. The trail continues through the trees for the Continental Divide Snowmobile Trail. Needless to say, we shared a good laugh.

Several times I rode into Christina Lake, but this also is the rough road route for vehicles. The trail along the road was strewn with boulders and rocks but not quite as bad as the road. The trail from Fiddler's Lake was definitely more enjoyable, although much longer. If I had the time, it was worth taking the longer route. I loved riding Liberty in new areas and I think it probably was more interesting to him, too.

PHOTOS

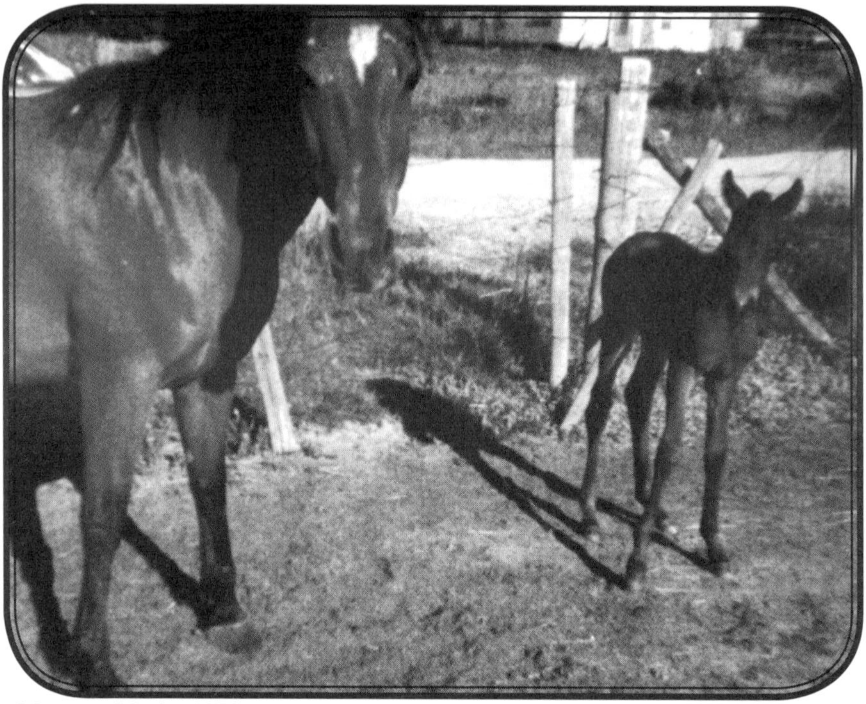

Missy and Babe 1979

Left to right: Babe, new born Dusty, Liberty and Missy

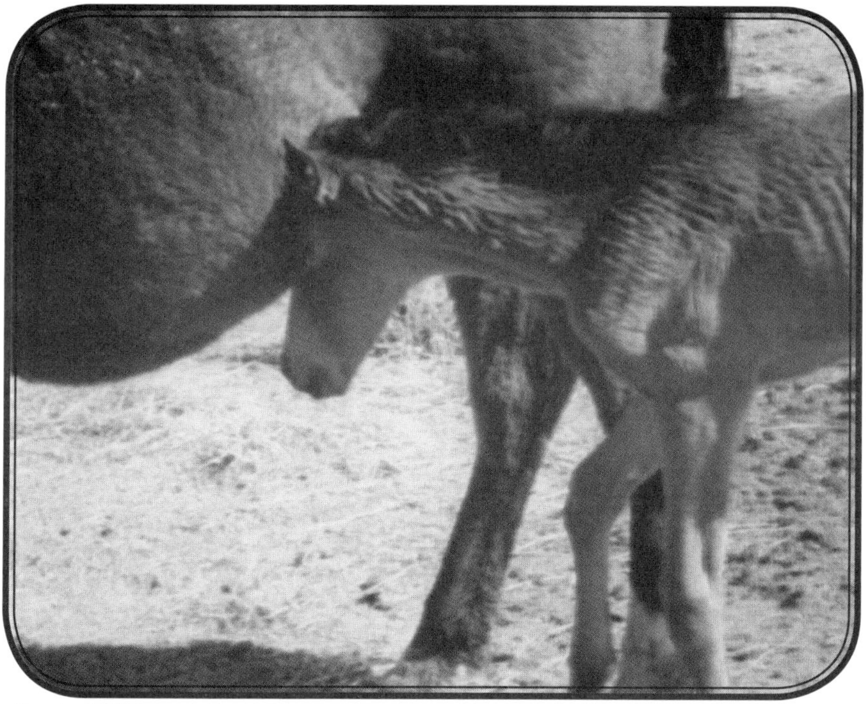

Sandy 1982

Wisconsin family on Babe, Missy and Liberty

Quarter Horse Family, Left to right: Dusty, Missy, Sandy, Liberty

Liberty's "1st use" of newly constructd Corral at Worthen Resivior. Constructed by Back Country Horsemen.

"Glad we don't have to go on THAT trail." Marston Pass 1986 or 1987, YNP Trip

Liberty, Missy, and Dusty at the end of Yellowstone/Marston Pass pack trip in 1986 or 1987.

Wyoming Centennial Wagon Train in 1990, Left to right: Dusty, Liberty, Missy

Wagon Train Picket Line 1990

Bureau of Land Management Sweetwater Canyon trip on Liberty with Sandy packing metal cages in 1993.

The Wyoming Centennial Wagon Train will Depart form Fort Caspar, Saturday, June 2, 1990.

Camp # 1	*— Poison Spider School Camp*	*12 miles*	*Saturday, June 2*
Camp # 2	*— Casper Creek Camp*	*12 miles*	*Sunday, June 3*
Camp # 3	*— Bedground Camp middle ford of Casper Creek*	*10 miles*	*Monday, June 4*
Camp # 4	*— Keg Springs Camp*	*11 miles*	*Tuesday, June 5*
Camp # 5	*— Hiland Reservoir Camp*	*12 miles*	*Wednesday, June 6*
Camp # 6	*— Hendry Camp*	*6 miles*	*Thursday, June 7*
Camp # 7	*— Rest Day at Hendry Camp*		*Friday, June 8*
Camp # 8	*— Lost Cabin Camp*	*15 miles*	*Saturday, June 9*
Camp # 9	*— Dolis Hill Camp*	*10 miles*	*Sunday, June 10*
Camp # 10	*— Bridger's Signature Camp*	*10 miles*	*Monday, June 11*
Camp # 11	*— Kirby Creek Camp*	*12 miles*	*Tuesday, June 12*
Camp # 12	*— Packsaddle Camp*	*12 miles*	*Wednesday, June 13*
Camp # 13	*— Stockman's Trail Camp*	*9 miles*	*Thrusday, June 14*
Camp # 14	*— Little Sand Draw Camp*	*9 miles*	*Friday, June 15*
Camp # 15	*— Worland Fairgrounds*	*14 miles*	*Saturday, June 16*
Camp # 16	*— Rest Day at Worland*		*Sunday, June 17*
Camp # 17	*— Murdock Cabin Camp*	*9 miles*	*Monday, June 18*
Camp # 18	*— Red Butte Camp*	*10 miles*	*Tuesday, June 19*
Camp # 19	*— Elk Creek Camp*	*9 miles*	*Wednesday, June 20*
Camp # 20	*— Painted Canyon Camp*	*5 miles*	*Thursday, June 21*
Camp # 21	*— Rest Day at Painted Canyon Camp*		*Friday, June 22*
Camp # 22	*— Rest Day at Painted Canyon Camp*		*Saturday, June 23*
Camp # 23	*— Burlington Camp*	*12 miles*	*Sunday, June 24*
Camp # 24	*— Emblem Stage and Freight Stop*	*10 miles*	*Monday, June 25*
Camp # 25	*— Coon Creek Camp*	*9 miles*	*Tuesday, June 26*
Camp # 26	*— Whistle Creek Camp*	*8 miles*	*Wednesday, June 27*
Camp # 27	*— Willwood Camp*	*8 miles*	*Thursday, June 28*
Camp # 28	*— Powell Fairgrounds*	*8 miles*	*Friday, June 29*
Camp # 29	*— Rest day at Powell*		*Saturday, June 30*
Camp # 30	*— Relocation Camp*	*11 miles*	*Sunday, July 1*
Camp # 31	*— Cody Stampede Grounds*	*11 miles*	*Monday, July 2*

Wyoming Centennial Wagon Train 1990.

Liberty on Oregon Trail 1993

Carol on Liberty, Sandy and myself at Bear Creek ride with Back Country Horsemen in 1995

Liberty at 19 years old, 1995

Liberty at Shoshone Lake at 20 years old, 1996

Liberty at Shoshone Lake at 20 years old, 1996

Carol and Liberty, Cody to Pahasha Ride 1996

Sandy led by Carole followed by Carol and Liberty on Pinnacles Trail opened by Back Country Horsemen in 1996.

Lora Davis, Wyoming Continental Divide Trail Guide author on Liberty at South Pass, circa 1997

Kathy Klein on Liberty on the Continental Divide Trail at South Pass, 1997

Sandy, Brandy and me at Fox Park near Yellowstone National Park boundary on the Continental Divide Trail in 1997

"Wild Horses!" South Pass Continental Divide Trail 1997

Pricey's first "picket out" at Double Cabins with Liberty 1998

Liberty and Pricey heading for her first river crossing at Double Cabins 1998.

John Bownson on Liberty the summer of 1998 at Monument Draw twenty miles round trip from Hudson.

John, Liberty, Pricey, Brandy and Carole, Rails to Trails, Heritage Trail ride with Paula, 1998

Game & Fish Expo Demo 1998

Carole Genaro, Summer 1999 "Packed Up" for week end trip on Liberty at Caldwaell Creek, Work trip from Double Cabins above Dubois. Liberty is 23 years old.

Lewis River Channel Trail in Yellowstone National Park, August 1999.

Yellowstone National Park Biscuit Basin Geysers Boardwalk, 1999

Yellowstone National Park geyser erupting near boardwalk that stopped Liberty, 1999.

Brandy the trail dog.

Brandy guarding Liberty while eating so other horses didn't get his "senior" feed.

Liberty & Sandy October 2001

Neighbor Joe's trailer of corn stalks, Dusty climbed in, 2002

Great looking 28 year old Liberty with younger trainee, Sassy, at Bruce's Corrals in 2004.

Liberty at 28 years old and Sassy taking in the view at the top of Fiarfield hill, during Squaw Creek Trail Mountain Education for Sassy the summer of 2004.

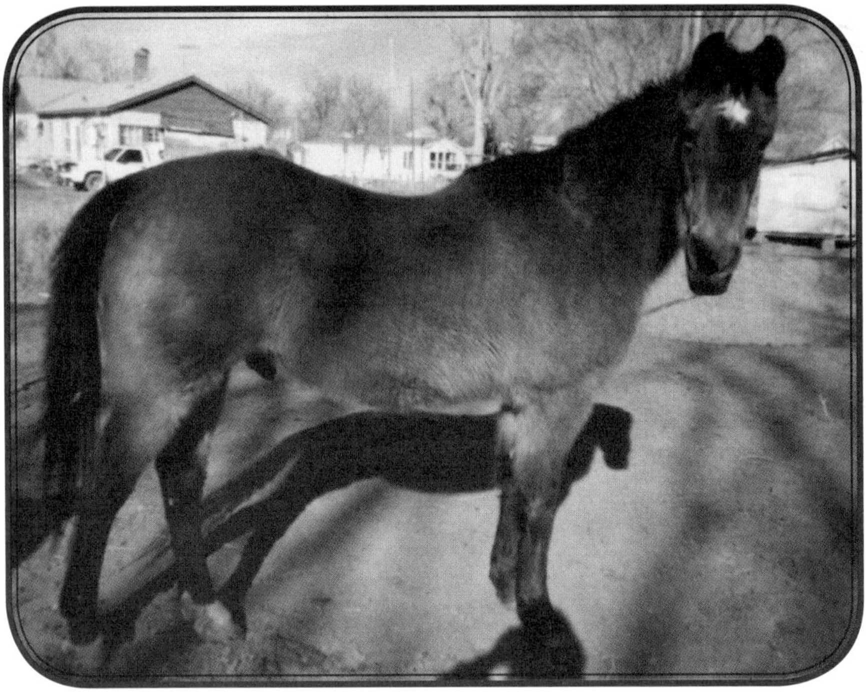

Liberty in Winter Coat at age 28, almost 29 in 2005.

Wyoming Centennial Wagon Train 1990, Sherry on her horse with pack horse.
Sandy, Liberty, Missy, Dusty, and Me. A ride into history.

8

CONTINENTAL DIVIDE NATIONAL SCENIC TRAIL

During the mid to latter 90's, the BCH, and I, individually, got involved with the Continental Divide Trail Alliance. The CDTA was charged with the task of locating and completing the 3100 mile Continental Divide National Scenic Trail that had been designated to run from the Mexico boundary to the Canada boundary. It had not been finished. Volunteers were invited to join the effort. I became involved through the BCH and also by myself. Our perspective was from the equine use view. At that time, the BCH was primarily interested in the mountain and forested areas, but I and a number of others were also interested in the high desert areas. My little trail dog, Shelly, had been gone for a number of years, but I now had a new, young, trail buddy, Brandy, a husky mix. She loved going anywhere with me and my horse. We went many, many, miles of trails as well as cross country travel. She was my CDT companion.

The first outing we did on the CDT was trail assessment from Turpin Meadows north to the southern boundary of Yellowstone Park. Our group of four traveled over a period of a week and took notes and pictures of the suggested route. I alternated riding and packing Liberty and Sandy. Our collected information was given to the CDTA for their analysis. My memories hold strong visuals of a wild and beautiful landscape. Brandy went the distance even though she was less than a year old.

Knowing the tentative route for the scenic trail crossed the Red Desert and Great Divide Basin from the Rawlins area, my interests also included the BLM and it's plans for their portions of the trail. I spent hours with Ray Hanson, the recreation planner who had just transferred from the Rawlins office to the Lander field office. He encouraged me to ride possible routes and report back to him with a perspective for equine travelers. Eventually, Ray became the Wyoming agency representative. He threw himself totally into locating and designating the route between the Medicine Bow and Shoshone National Forests. I was thrilled to be a part of the process. My enjoyment of and interest in high desert terrain was shared by several of my riding companions. We formed a small group to focus our attention on those particular sections of the trail and called ourselves Lander Desert Riders. Liberty and I were starting to spend lots of time on the CDT all over Wyoming.

A work project scheduled by the CDTA was at Green River Lakes. I was signed up for it and eagerly planned and prepared to attend. The volunteers would pitch tents to camp at the first lake's campground. From there we would work on the trail to the west the first day and to the east a small bridge was to be constructed. Our work crew consisted of forest service employees, CDTA crew leaders, and a number of volunteers which included a newspaper reporter grandmother and her grandson. Our diverse bunch had a great time.

I had brought Liberty along so I could ride on the trail after our project was finished. We were the first travelers to cross over the new bridge and I totally enjoyed seeing some new country on down the trail. Liberty munched grass in a beautiful meadow as I marveled at the majestic view of a prominent landmark, Square Top Mountain, which has appeared on the Wyoming road map as well as in several documentaries.

From Green River Lakes the trail continues northwesterly and eventually tops over in the Sheridan Creek area. A group of

BCHA members were going to the area to try to locate a possible route between Sheridan Pass and on northwesterly to Pilot Knob near Togwotee Pass where the trail would cross the highway. I couldn't go on the day they decided on but I wanted to participate. I called one of them that evening and got a summary of their experiences.

On my next free day, I drove up past Dubois with my van and trailer and Liberty. Turning off the highway I headed up a dirt two track, parked, and saddled up. The area was rough and rocky as we left the two track trail and headed for Sheridan Pass. There were a few flagged places as we worked our way up through the jumble of rock, trees, downfall, and some human made gravel bed flue areas. Then we were stopped by a wall of small, closely growing trees that, try as we may, we could not penetrate.

Backtracking numerous times and turning different directions with Liberty, I concluded I really wasn't sure which direction to go to try to continue on or even return to the trailer. "OK, Liberty, get us out of here". Turning and walking with purpose, Liberty took over and we were soon back in a recognizable area. I turned him back into the trees to try to find another way through. Again and again we ended up in a mess and would return to our last known "trail flagged" point.

Clouds were beginning to look threatening and the wind was picking up. It was time to give up and return another time. By the time we got to the trailer it was raining pretty hard and I was glad we quit when we did.

I stopped at a restaurant a few miles back down the highway and sat at a window that faced the forested area we had been in. Lightening bolts flashed and thunder crashed over the area. I was really glad to be out of there. I later learned there had been a funnel cloud sighted, which was rare for the area. That information made me REALLY glad I had left when I did.

During this time period, I was involved with the CDT in a number of ways. I spent many hours horseback in the South Pass area and, eventually, I rode the route across the part of the Red Desert south of Jeffrey City and on to Rawlins. As I became more familiar with the route, Ray, my BLM contact, asked if I would consider taking a certain person horseback from Bison Basin road across to South Pass City. Lora Davis had been contracted with the Alliance to write the guide book for the Wyoming portion of the Trail. She had hiked, biked, trekked with lamas and goats, backpacked, and driven the trail route beginning from the Colorado border to the Bison Basin Road. I was to meet her at the crossing point on the road with my horses and she would ride horseback for two days with me to South Pass City.

I was thrilled with anticipation. My Liberty would take good care of her. We had no problem packing our camping items as both Liberty and Sandy were well conditioned to the task. Lora and I hit it off immediately and we covered the distance with no problems. Arriving in the South Pass area, we spent time exploring the hills and speculating where the trail would pass through. Lora continued heading west and I returned home. Thus began a friendship that continues to this day.

A temporary routing of the CDT trail would have had the traveler experiencing a number of hours in the bar pit along the highway 287 north of Rawlins. I decided to see what that experience would be like for a horse back rider. I never dreamed it would be as awful as it was. Not only was it horrible, it was really dangerous. Steady traffic included semi trucks, buses, recreational vehicles, cars, and trucks. The fences were close to the road in places and diverted up to the pavement around culverts. Where the bar pit was wider, most often it had standing water on top of questionable ground. I was riding Sandy and he was as hyper as could be. I sometimes yearned for my super reliable Liberty as we navigated our way through mud, water, sand, "moonscape looking terrain", and every imaginable as well as UNIMAGINABLE piece of garbage and trash possible. This is an area of "dead" soil and moisture, as it does not drain. The divide splits and separates into two rims and then comes back together. Along the bar pit was broken glass, cans, coolers, lids, cardboard, boxes, tarps, blankets, wire, rope, appliances, furniture, pipe, metal, luggage, carcasses and bones, vehicle parts, tires, wood, toys, papers, (what have I missed!) You name it. Sandy and I were on pins and needles for a good 10 miles. At the bottom of the 9 mile hill, we were able to find a place to walk that was further from the road bed and had only sporadic trash to avoid.

Before starting out on this highway stretch, I had made phone calls, written letters, and tried to interest others in checking out this route. One contact I had been steered to was a Rawlins resident who was active in volunteer work and also was a "horse person". Bill assured me he would meet up with me along the highway and we would continue on into Rawlins on our horses. After topping over the big hill, a slight down grade and a more diverse, vegetated terrain was a welcome sight. A truck pulling a horse trailer whizzed by with the driver waving wildly. I waited while Bill found a place to turn around at the bottom of the hill, and soon he was back and unloading his saddled horse. After a brief visit to get acquainted, we rode toward Rawlins. A short rain and lightning storm hurried us along. On top of that open flat was no place to be riding a leisurely pace in that weather.

Through my volunteering on the CDT, new friendships developed. Through Bill, I was introduced to other "horse persons", including Rich. We began riding more of the trail south of Rawlins. Sometimes Rich and I couldn't coordinate our time off and I often rode by myself. Other times, especially on holiday weekends, Bill and family, Rich, and others, even Lora, and I would meet up somewhere along the CDT and camp together. We had great rides and great times. My information was passed on to Ray and it helped guide decisions about trail locations for the CDT. My report about the awful bar pit ride and my suggestion for a cross country route were instrumental in getting that part of the route changed.

Working around my work schedule, I drove down past Rawlins many times to ride the CDT. One weekend found me camped near the entry into the Medicine Bow/Routt National Forest. On a quiet, serenely beautiful hillside, I contemplated how fortunate I was to be in this place of total peace. Sipping my coffee the next morning, I actually found it quite difficult to get motivated to leave. One of those special places, it easily comes to mind.

Another memorable area nearby was a wildlife sanctuary the trail goes right through. Further on south, near Hog Park, (how it got that name, I haven't a clue) the route crossed roads to nearby popular recreation areas. Eventually I rode the trail to the Colorado border. Riding the nearby trails introduced me to more new country, something I always enjoy. Some of my most enjoyable riding and camping experiences took place south of Rawlins. I have really pleasant feelings when I think about the Sierra Madres.

Actually, it is very difficult for me to pick one favorite place or area out of my many memories. Some places or events are extremely pleasant, exciting, scary, disagreeable, or just memorable. A ride in the Pacific Creek area falls into the "learning" category. Liberty and I headed east out of the campground. The main trail continued to a crossing of the river. At the water's edge, Liberty stopped and surveyed the crossing. I urged him forward. He entered the water, then stopped and began to turn around. No, I wanted to go on.

After some testing of our wills, he went on and all of sudden, down into a hole we went. He had been able to sense a change in the river bottom. I had insisted on him continuing on when he could tell something wasn't right. I gave him his head and hung on. He floundered until he got turned around back on some good footing and on out of the river. I should have checked out why he had balked. Looking around, I saw a fainter trail that stayed out of the river but continued in the right direction. We followed it and enjoyed the rest of our outing with no other mishaps. Probably moose were still using the route into the river and on through some boggy willows. That use would keep the trail fresh looking. The better trail for us just wasn't so visibly apparent. There would be many "learning" situations in the future.

Liberty was now in his 20's and the babies were all teenagers. I had put my Babe down when she was 21 because she was so arthritic my heart broke to see her in such pain. How long would Liberty enjoy good health was a question that entered my thoughts often. And along the same line, what were my plans for continuing my horse use. It takes time to start a new horse and, furthermore, I didn't want to bring just any horse into my equine family. I knew I would want to commit myself to any additional animal, but I had no desire to just go out and buy any old horse. I certainly didn't want an animal that I would be comparing to my Liberty. I already knew he was one of a kind and no other would ever measure up. A new horse for me would have to be "special". A hard decision but I didn't have to make it yet.

9
WILD HORSES

During the rides on the desert trails, I often saw or heard about wild horses. These mustangs were managed by the BLM. Periodic roundups were held to manage the numbers and some of them were sent to the Wyoming Prison Honor Farm north of Riverton. A new program involved select inmates working with the horses to gentle them and make them more desirable for purchase. Buyers were allowed to draw a number to determine when it would be their turn to pick a horse. They could buy it for $125. The sales were held in the hopes that many mustangs would find good homes. I never went to one of them. Who would want to pick from what was left? Not me.

A new neighbor moved into an adjoining property on the north side of me. He instantly fell in love with my horses. Would I let him spend time with them and maybe even help him learn to ride sometime? John and I began a friendship that included hours and hours with the horses. He liked Liberty a lot and rode him many times. His favorite, though, was little, red, Dusty. John would press his face against his cheek and look into Dusty's eye and laugh with glee. He even did a metal carving of Dusty's head and sent it to his Dad for a gift. John loved Dusty, but he enjoyed all of my horses. One day he saw me working Missy in harness and came over to watch. Pretty soon he wanted to try and later I took pictures of him and he took some of me. Missy was just bored with it all, but we had a great time.

I had told John about my increasing anxiety over what the future might hold for my continuing horse use. How could I bring a strange horse into my family? They were part of my family. Robin was in Salt Lake City and doing a great job of living her life. My horses were with me everyday. They ARE my family, too. Bringing in an outsider didn't seem right. But, if I wanted to go on riding for the foreseeable future, I needed to be working with some younger horse.

At some point in time, I heard about an upcoming sale at the honor farm with some very major changes to how it would be conducted. Instead of drawing a number for a place in line to pick out an animal, they auctioned each animal. The sale sounded interesting and I asked John if he wanted to go. I had no intentions, I just wanted to see how it worked. It would be fun to see what the animals would bring and I would enjoy seeing some close up. Until then, I had only seen them from quite a distance away and often they were on the run.

I have some pictures from a ride I was on that began in South Pass City. I had run into two gals, one from England, the other from Australia, at the Pacific Creek trailhead. They were riding and packing from Canada to Mexico on the CDT. After a lengthy visit, we agreed to meet at South Pass and I would ride with them to Rawlins. I had been riding Liberty at Pacific Creek but I rode Sandy from South Pass across the high mountain desert country. Sandy had become my long distance horse. He is so smooth at a fast walk or trot, the miles just fly.

The picture I mentioned shows the gals riding ahead of me and in the distance, a herd of wild horses that would split into smaller bands, then several bands would combine back into a large mass of moving animals. We saw every size, color, and description! Young colts ran alongside their moms. Older, single, sometimes injured, animals struggled to keep up. The moving spectacle made me catch my breath and the girls hollered excitedly over their shoulders. As our path of travel circled around and in front of the herd, the horses often stopped and stared with nervous curiosity. We passed by the last of them, and silently thanked them for the beautiful and inspiring demonstration of wild freedom they had shown us. I was totally blown away. Memories of Liberty doing laps around the pasture when I first turned him loose flooded my mind then, and even now.

John and I went to the honor farm sale. We walked around the outside of the corral where the horses to be sold were tied up so prospective buyers could look them over at close range. Inmates stood by ready to answer questions about an animal's temperament and how they had responded to the gentling process so far. Notes were being jotted down by the description and listing of each horse in the sale brochure. I put an "x" by horses that impressed me for some reason. It would be fun to see what they sold for. One horse was just a year old according to the brochure. She was long winter haired and almost black. As she stuck her nose up to the corral pole, John reached out to pat it and instantly declared she was the cutest thing he had ever seen. As we moved around the corral, some horses pawed and flicked their ears, showing their nervousness and impatient nature.

We came to another black, long haired filly. She was just over a year old and stood back on her lead rope looking at us with a frightened, steady stare. Standing on long straight legs, her beautiful head had the biggest, mysterious, black eyes. Looking into them seemed like looking into pitch black pools. I made several marks by her number in the brochure. A couple other horses impressed me enough to make a mark by their number.

The auction began and most of the horses sold for the opening minimum bid of $125. Some didn't sell and they would be rescheduled for the next sale. Some horses were barely gentle. Others were saddled and a few were ridden in. The black filly I had been so impressed with was led in. Obviously very frightened, she none the less followed the inmate. My heart went out to her. When the bidding began, my hand went up in the air seemingly by itself, along with half a dozen other hands. What was I doing? The bidding bounced around the spectators, and a few dropped out. It was down to me and one other person. The bidding went back and forth and presently it went over $300. I must be crazy. As it turned out to be, I was totally entranced with her, just like I had been with Liberty. The other bidder stopped and I held my breath as I looked at the auctioneer. Applause broke out as he announced she was sold to me. I looked at John and almost broke into tears.

More horses were brought in and some sold. The small filly was led in and the announcer made comments about what a great gift she would be for your child or grandchild. She was small but I knew she could grow up to be a great horse as my Dusty had. John grabbed my arm and started telling me all the reasons why he thought I should buy her, too. I bid on her and it ended with me buying her, too!

I had many arrangements to make, including calling a friend with the right kind of enclosed horse trailer to haul them home and figuring out how to pay for them. They hadn't advertised it, but they were able to process credit card sales. I was relieved. It all worked out and it was obviously meant to be. My first pick turned out to bring the second highest amount bid of the sale. I hadn't been the only one to tune into her potential. She lives up to it all.

I had gone to the sale to see how it worked and to see what qualities the horses had. I was so impressed with how good the animals looked. They were definitely not "broom tailed nags". Many were fine boned, well muscled, or put together with beautiful confirmation. Some showed the mustang heritage of strength and endurance. Take your pick, all the various qualities were present in varying degrees. Pricey Blue Light Special, (guess how she got her name) was described as a blue roan. After a couple years, her colors and patterns did indeed show she was. Sassy, (originally called Friendly but changed as she showed her mischievous nature) was also technically described as a blue roan. She eventually would be almost totally white, with her winter coat on and almost a light tweed of dark dots in her summer coat. Sandy had turned all different colors for his first couple years before getting his permanent buckskin color so the girls' colors didn't surprise me too much.

Introduction of the girls into my family of horses turned out to be easier than I anticipated. Because Pricey was very apprehensive with just about everything, I needed to go slow with her and gain her trust and confidence. I kept the girls in the corral the first few days. I had taken the halter off her when I turned her loose and she would move away from me if I approached. When I noticed her lying down, I slowly walked to the edge of the pole corral. Getting down on my hands and knees, talking softly, I crept closer to her. If she started looking from side to side, a sign of distress, I stopped.

Eventually, I reached out my hand and touched her nose. She smelled me and I began to work my way around her face, neck, shoulder, and down her back. I worked back to her head and made sure she smelled, heard, and felt me. I even blew my breath to her as I intently looked into her eyes. We had the beginnings of bonding! She had shown a great deal of trust and I was very aware of it. We had begun the process of bringing new horses into our family. New adventures were just around the corner.

Liberty once again was recruited to help me in my work with horses. Sassy, originally named Friendly, was true to her original name, but, as time went by, she became more aware of her ability to bully Missy and Pricey. She would stand up to Dusty and Sandy and not give ground. When it came to Liberty, there was no question. He was BOSS. He didn't have to do more than flick his ears back and she got the message. She played with him but didn't challenge him at all.

When I first put the girls into the same pasture with the others, some running and chasing took place. Pecking order was getting established. The girls stayed by themselves for a few days, then began to mingle with the others.

A couple of lessons were learned over a period of time. Brandy was always around when I worked or spent time with any of the horses. Mustangs equate dogs, especially husky looking ones like Brandy, with coyotes. Sassy would even chase Brandy and try to strike her with her front hooves or whirl around and try to nail her from the back. Brandy always kept her eye on Sassy and could read her intentions. Sassy was adept at turning and literally running backwards before letting both hind feet fly. I couldn't help but admire her agility.

An airplane flying low or, especially, a helicopter flying nearby would send the girls off at a gallop to get away. Memories of their capture were slow to go away. Many times I observed the girls watching the other horses to see if they should react. More and more, the girls stayed within the safety of their new herd.

I began to take one of the girls for walks around town, leading her while I rode Liberty. He seemed to sense how frightened they were of all the new sights and sounds we encountered. He was so good for me when I needed to concentrate on keeping the whole situation under control. His behavior would directly influence the horse we were ponying and soon a crises was averted. One time I took Sassy out with the pack saddle and box panniers. As we went along, Sassy was so busy looking everywhere for "horse eating monsters", she continually banged the hard surfaces of the boxes against Liberty's butt and side. He patiently walked along. She would learn. She did.

As Sassy seemed to be adjusting to being handled and was doing well, I worked more with Pricey. The trips around town progressed to longer ones out on the BLM. She has an easier way of going about her and doesn't panic or get rattled. Something might spook her but she checks it out instead of reacting first. Sassy has since outgrown that spooking habit. Pricey learned a lot of ground work and with that we advanced to saddling and tacking up. She had increasing trust and before long I was on her back. John would ride Liberty and we went along cueing from Liberty's behavior.

John and Liberty were good partners for Pricey and me. Rides were often and very enjoyable. I especially value the memory of the first time we rode out past the cattle guard and onto open BLM land. It was a real achievement and John took a good picture of me on Pricey.

Another memorable trip was when John and I met Paula, another long time riding friend, north of Riverton and rode across the formidable Old Black Bridge on the Heritage Trail which uses the Rails to Trails route to Shoshoni. John decided to walk and lead Liberty across the bridge even though I assured him Liberty had crossed over it before. Pricey hardly hesitated and cautiously walked across. Paula had to coach her horse for awhile and eventually she succeeded in riding across. No face lost, it's a pretty scary crossing, whether you decide to ride or walk.

BCH planned a weekend at what is known as Double Cabins, a beautiful open meadow on Wiggins Fork, north of Dubois. A fenced-in forest service campground for campers and trailers, as well as a number of corrals and lots of primitive, open and secluded camp sites, were available for use. I decided Pricey was ready to be introduced to the mountains. I would take Liberty also so I could ride him and pony her.

On the first ride, several riders crossed a wide area of the river to access a certain trail and I followed on Liberty and led her. Pricey planted her feet at the water's edge and wouldn't budge. I moved from side to side to try to get her to step into the swift moving river. Several times I rode Liberty back out of the water and then entered it again, trying to show her it was okay.

One of the riders, Al, called out to me, "take a wrap around your saddle horn and have Liberty pull her in". I could only pray she didn't jump right on top of us. As Liberty pulled her off balance, she made a giant leap towards us and Liberty moved sideways. As she splashed into the water, she calmly began walking behind Liberty as if that had been what she had been doing all along. It had been scary and dramatic but it had no aftermaths.

She had no problems entering or crossing any water after that. Indeed, to this day, she loves to go into ponds or water crossings to splash with her legs and hooves, and swing her nose and face back and forth under the water. Often those watching warn me she might be getting ready to lay down in the water but she never has. She just likes to play in the water and it's fun to watch. On hot days it feels pretty good to both of us.

By Sunday afternoon most of our group had left, except Jack, and he and I went for a ride. The relatively flat terrain was easy going and I had left Liberty tied up at camp. Pricey and I were leading and we came to a wide, washed out gully. The steep, narrow trail down the side to the left made a hairpin turn to the right. I assumed Pricey would follow the trail to the right but instead she tried to go up the bank ahead of her. My weight and the soft dirt caused her to slide back, and down on her butt she went. My feet were out of the stirrups in a flash so she wouldn't land on me. She lay on her side without moving as I talked quickly and quietly to her, and I crawled around to the front and got to my feet. Encouraging her to get up, I answered Jack's frantic calls. He later told me from behind it looked like I just disappeared.

Pricey's bad choice was as much my fault as hers. I needed to remember that she would learn to make better decisions in the future and I needed to help her with that. I continued on the ride with resolve to not take so much for granted. Liberty was happy to see us returning, and he and Pricey called loudly to each other. I was thankful that the ride ended on such a positive note. The weekend had been pretty eventful and more memories were stored.

It was fun to take both Liberty and Pricey on outings, long or short. Pricey got more experience and learned from being with my old reliable friend. I would alternate riding him with her and leading the other. I took them both down to the Battle Pass area several times. Bill or Rich, and their friends, would be camping. We would find them and have an enjoyable weekend. I learned more of the area and I was able to ride all of the CDT down there.

One time it had rained a couple days before we were to meet. Rich said he would meet me on the graveled road and pull my horse trailer into the camp area. We were both pretty sure I would spin out on the damp hill going in, as my van didn't have 4- wheel drive. Without the trailer I was fine. We got into the camp area, unloaded the horses, tied them to the trailer, and Rich unhooked from it. All of my horses are trained to lead up and along with any vehicle they are connected to. As we sat and visited, catching up on gossip, I caught sight of movement of my trailer. One of them had probably pulled on their lead rope hard enough to reach grass and the trailer had moved. The other would think the trailer was on the move so was leading up on it. The end result was the two horses were slowly pulling the trailer forward! After we got them and it stopped, and my van hooked back on, we had a good laugh. Not so funny at first but now that everything was okay, it was pretty hilarious to remember.

Talking with Rich one day, we decided to do a day ride to Shoshone Lake. It was a pleasant 7 mile ride from Dickinson Park to the lake and now it would b a good way to initiate Sassy to mountain travel. I would ride Liberty and lead Sassy. I brought the pack saddle along and put it on her. She was already used to it. I didn't put any packs on as she would have enough to occupy her thoughts along the way.

The trail had not been used much in recent years. Most travelers to the lake were now using the Squaw Creek 4 wheeler track, or as a last resort, the nightmare road route over Cyclone Pass. Many times we had to detour around downfall. One place looked like pick up sticks had been played with the trees. The horses stepped and hopped over and around the obstacles. We came to a large tree trunk across the trail. Large rocks prevented an easy detour around it. As Liberty carefully got over it, I wondered if Sassy would balk and pull back. She nimbly jumped right over it. If Liberty got over it, she could, too. She tracked right along with Liberty and presently we were within sight of the lake. Rich wanted to get an early start home, so, we enjoyed the view for awhile, then we turned and headed back up the trail.

It would be the last time I would take Liberty to our special place. As he was at a somewhat mature stage of his life by then, I am always thankful we were able to do that ride. I am fortunate to have so many memories of such a beautiful area. The longer horse trip from the south or the grind up the road from Trout Creek are both worth the effort.

The pastures near my house had become pretty sparse and the horses all decided to look for "greener pastures". Sometime after their evening ration of hay, they found a weak fence area and all of them got out. In the morning I discovered them missing and started driving around. I found my quarter horse family all together and by catching up Liberty and leading him home, I was able to coax the others to follow. The mustang girls were not with them. I drove up and down all over Hudson. No one had seen them and I had no idea where they might go.

Eventually, I ended up looking over a fence that separated town property from BLM land. A herd of horses were grazing nearby, and in the midst of them were my girls. How they found their way into that area and into that herd of domestic horses is a mystery. Now, how to get them back!

I climbed through the fence and approached the girls. A dominant horse zoomed over and chased the girls away from me.

The herd moved further away. After several attempts to quietly get up to Pricey, I gave up. The other horses were not letting me get close to my girls. I needed Liberty. By the time I caught him up, saddled him, and rode him to where the horses had been, the herd had moved a long way. As we reached them, Liberty called the girls. They answered him and attempted to come but were cut off by the other horses.

Several times I was able to cut them out of the herd and then I would lose them as the herd surrounded us and took the girls back. Liberty rose to the situation and became more aggressive. Finally we were successful and made our way to a nearby gate. After we got through the gate, I put a halter and lead rope on Pricey and led her home, with Sassy following close by. She really did not want to be left behind! When we reached home, a happy reunion ensued. Everyone was happy to see everyone.

On another occasion the outcome was not readily positive. I had made plans to meet Lora at a camp that Bill and his wife had invited me to for the Labor Day weekend. It rained on me as I pulled my trailer (with Pricey in it) into the camp. On and off, it rained almost the whole time we were there. It cleared for a very short time and I managed to squeeze in a 20 minute ride down to a creek crossing and back before the weather socked in again. We spent a lot of time in their camper and my van that weekend. Of the many times I went down there, this was the most miserable. Pricey spent the whole time on a high line. The lead rope she was hooked on with had a big, heavy clip and no swivel. The rope ended up all twisted and several times I undid it to straighten it out. It was soaked and starting to fray apart.

The weather hadn't improved so everyone decided to leave early on the last day. I was just about ready to load Pricey and, as I looked over at her, I could see her rope had come apart and she was munching grass. I headed for her and she took off into some trees. I couldn't keep up with her, and Lora, coming up the trail, said she had headed down towards the creek crossing we had ridden to. I ran back and asked Bill if I could ride the extra horse he had brought. He said it didn't know much but I could use it.

Off we went on our horses trying to follow Pricey's hoof prints. Down at the creek area it was really a boggy mess. Bill had had enough and the horse I had been on wouldn't cross the boggy area. Back at camp, we agreed to meet the following weekend if I hadn't gotten her back yet. Lora and I kept looking and calling till late afternoon, but, without horses, it was pretty futile. Lora and I gave up for the day. Late Monday afternoon, she went back to her home in Colorado and I drove home with my empty trailer. Sick with worry, I consoled myself with plans to return and find her the next weekend.

Friday came and I headed back to Battle Pass with my faithful friend, Liberty, in the trailer. Bill was under the weather and couldn't come. I wasn't familiar with the area that Pricey's tracks had headed into and Bill had said there was a big canyon she may have gone down into. I needed Liberty. He didn't have shoes on and hadn't been out much, but he was in pretty good shape.

I unloaded Liberty in the parking area along the Battle Pass highway as another vehicle pulled in. It was a Carbon County deputy sheriff and we began to visit. I explained the situation to him and he promised he would keep an eye out and let me know if he spotted her. This was his regular patrol area and he was bound to see or hear of her as he spent most of his time here. I slept good with positive thoughts of seeing Pricey soon.

Saturday morning I was saddled up and heading down the trail early. As we passed the area we had been camped at, I hopefully scanned the area. It was too much to hope for, but it would have been fantastic to see her grazing in the meadow. Down the trail we went until we reached the creek. I had no idea if she had kept going along the edge of the meadow or if she had dropped down into the canyon that parallels the trail I had come down.

I rode on along the trail for a ways as it traveled through open terrain, calling her name and hoping Liberty would pick up her sound or scent and call out. I didn't see any fresh manure or hoof prints. Her feet were hard as a rock and she didn't need shoes so her prints would be different. We reached a point where I could use my "one eye", a single, magnifying sighting lens, and I scanned as far ahead as I could. Seeing nothing, I decided to backtrack and find the trail Bill had said led down into the canyon.

We were now going into unknown territory and I felt thankful and confident riding my reliable, old friend. We spent a long time in that canyon and I decided that we needed to be getting back to the trailer. It would take a long time to turn around and return the way we had come. Surely, we must be at the far end of the canyon and up over the rim would be a far quicker way. I saw several possible routes and we began to try to go up to the top. Again and again, Liberty fought his way up through rock, stubby vegetation, and steep terrain. We were stopped by ledges, boulders, and eventually a multi wired fence. Liberty seemed to realize we were trying to go back to where the van and trailer were and he was trying his darnedest to do it. He definitely was giving his all.

In the end, I turned him back down to the trail and we headed back the way we came. I was pooped by the time we reached the trailer and van. I felt bad for Liberty, he had tried so hard. The next time I talked to Bill, he said he didn't think it was possible to come out of the canyon that way, even on foot. I had to agree with him. We rode another trail on Sunday, but didn't travel too far and saw nothing. A few people riding and some hiking said they hadn't seen or heard of Pricey. With a heavy heart I headed home.

I continued checking with any agencies, as well as any individuals I could think of, that might have information. I talked on the phone with the deputy almost every day. He told me a dispatcher for the Rawlins police department had reported seeing Pricey while she had been camping. She had actually gotten up to Pricey and taken the clip and ragged piece of rope off of the halter so it couldn't get caught on something. For some reason she didn't have Pricey but had been convinced that she would hang around the area. The deputy checked the area but, as a few days had passed before he heard the report, she was no where to be found.

My neighbors wanted to see some of that area so the next weekend the three of us went down using their pickup to pull my trailer. It had rained and they had 4 wheel drive. We ran into the deputy who suggested areas we could check out. With no new information or leads, my trailer came home empty. Where was she?

The next week began as usual. I was at work when a call came from the deputy. He had spotted her just as it was getting dark and he and his friend would catch her that afternoon after work. He said to not worry about coming down until the weekend so I wouldn't miss any work. They would put Pricey in a corral in town and he would feed and water her till I picked her up. I was so happy and relieved. How strange it had been, though, when he questioned how big she was and that she was thinner than I had described.

My relief drained away the next morning when he called me to say he didn't have my blue roan. He had somebody else's red roan. When they caught it up, they realized it was not Pricey. He was so sorry he had gotten my hopes up. Now he felt like it was personal. He promised he would find her. He did as he said. A couple days later he called and said "I have YOUR horse. I'm holding her right now. And you are right, she IS big and in good shape. Come get her this weekend. I'll take care of her till then."

I wonder who the other horse belonged to and what ever happened to it. Some vegetables from my garden plus my full gratitude found their way to a house in Encampment. All my horses were happy to be reunited. Liberty was right up front to sniff noses with Pricey and welcome her back.

10
FLASHBACKS

Liberty was ridden by my best friend, Carol, more than by anyone else, other than myself. She got along with him so good and he was so predictable for her. We rode out on the BLM a lot. Carol was one of the Lander Desert Riders and she was riding Liberty with us as six of us surveyed a section of the CDT east of South pass. It was pretty hot that day and we were all drinking our water regularly as we went along. I reminded Carol to drink and she assured me she was.

We were more than half way for the distance to be covered to reach the trailer for our ride home. Carol began to fall behind and I urged her to make Liberty stay up. She did but soon she was falling behind again. I got behind Liberty and smacked him on the butt and as she told me he was trying, she didn't sound right. Soon she said she didn't feel very good. As I asked her about how much water she drank, she held up her small canteen of water, which was about half full. She said she had a headache and felt dizzy.

Calling out to the others, I helped her get down to sit on the ground. In my saddlebags I had what I hoped she needed. She was getting dehydrated and the elevation compounded her condition.

In a packet I had gotten from the CDTA, as a volunteer, was an envelope of electrolytes powder. I put it into my bottle of water and filled it up with the balance of her water. Even though she had become nauseated, she sipped it and presently got it all down. After awhile, she was able to get up and we got her back in the saddle.

Bill, one of the Lander Desert Riders, had hot footed down the trail to the trailer and was able to follow two tracks to drive almost all the way back to us. By the time we met, Carol was doing much better and we loaded up to head home. The electrolytes had done the job and she was thankful I had given it to her. I was thankful I had it in my saddlebag, thanks to the vendors who donate the items to the Alliance for volunteer projects. Liberty had been a good boy through it all. No acting up or taking advantage of her.

As good as Liberty tended to be, he did have some annoying habits. If you happened to be standing near his head, when you least expected it, he would jam his nose into your back, shoulder, or wherever he could reach, and almost knock you off your feet. If you were facing him, he aimed for your chest. He wasn't trying to hurt, he just wanted to get on with whatever, just showing his impatient side. Sometimes I thought this "bumping" was more like a game to him. If you ignored him, he would likely do it again. During all the years I had him, he never ever bumped me in the face.

Another way for him to try to get my attention, and tell me he thought he should get fed, was for him to work on the old, jeep truck door. I have the bed of the truck sticking into the pasture at the place where I throw hay. That way the whole bunch could get at the hay I threw into the bed without pushing each other around. The old truck was shot and the driver's door was sprung so it didn't shut all the way. Liberty would push the door open and closed with his nose. Most of the time it made a loud noise and it tended to get a response out of me. This action of his usually got a laugh out of me.

I had spent many hours horseback on both Liberty and Sandy while volunteering for the CDTA and BLM. Many of my trips involved camping overnight and sometimes two nights under the open sky. I enjoyed the challenge of figuring out meals that would carry me through the three days. My "Horse packing with no pack horse" skills got better with use.

Several years had passed since I began working with Ray at the BLM. One day he told me he had nominated me for an award to be given at the National Trail Symposium in Tucson, Arizona. I would be recognized for my volunteer work with Wyoming's BLM. I had been selected and the trip to receive the award was to be part of the award. Ray was to receive an award also so he would be there along with other state and agency officials. WOW, I was so happy!

We attended seminars and at one session, we were approached by a gal from Oregon who also was there to receive an award. She was by herself and asked if she could hang out with us. We hit it off right away. She was a horse person, too, and did the "no pack horse thing" regularly. We all had the best time and Becky and I became fast friends. We agreed to write back and forth and send pictures to each other. She was in Back Country Horsemen of Oregon and did lots of volunteering. We were like kindred spirits. We exchanged stories of our animals and experiences with them. Years later, Becky came to Wyoming several times and we camped and rode together Our friendship is strong and wonderful.

On her first trip to Wyoming after we met, Becky brought two girl friends from Oregon with her. They were scheduled to go on a catered ride on the "Hole in the wall" trail, ending in Thermopolis. Arriving in Wyoming a week early, Becky planned to spend time at the Turpin Meadows trail head and I was eager to see her again and meet her friends. They had all brought their own horses and we would ride some of the trails in the vicinity.

As it turned out, one of the friends, Angie, was building a summer home west of Dubois. The location she had chosen was a very short distance from where my cousin Gary, friend Jim, and I had experienced the drama of my being stuck on the rock during the hunting trip years earlier. Angie's place is just a few lots from my "hero", Tim's place. He had lost his wife and moved to Oregon, near where Angie lived. Tim and Angie were friends. What a small world!

Becky and I rode a long way one of the days and we enjoyed catching up on each other's activities. We rode up the south fork of the Buffalo. Going east on the Soda Fork trail, we reached a trail junction that had a neat old cabin. We took lots of pictures and had our lunch. The area is home to many bears, including grizzlies, but apparently they were in their day beds as we saw only sign. Our horses were aware the bears were in the vicinity, though.

We talked about the CDT and I suggested we travel up to South Pass and ride on some of the trail. We stopped in Lander to see Ray at the BLM office and told him where we were going, which pleased him very much. We did a quick "express" tour of South Pass City and rode the trail which passes through the restored town. Our camp for the evening was just outside of town and we rode horseback into the setting sun for a couple of miles. A "Kodak moment" turned into one of the most treasured pictures I have. I went home and back to work, but I was able to be in Thermopolis to meet the girls after their "Hole in the wall" ride. They headed back to Oregon, all of us vowing to stay in touch.

Over the years my horses were pastured in many areas around Hudson. At one point I was at a loss to find a place all of them could be together. I contacted the owner of a pasture just out of town that was ten acres with an irrigation canal running across it. The owner's son had several horses in it but I could put mine in there until I found something else. I knew mine would stay together and off by themselves. This proved to be partially true.

A rank gelding dominated the other herd and he was determined to make my mares his. Often people would tell me they had seen the horses chasing each other around the pasture, sometimes rearing and fighting. I was upset to find Missy with bite marks and cuts on her. A couple days later, Dusty also had some signs of fighting on him. He was marked up more than Missy.

A few days later a neighbor driving past saw Liberty and the gelding fighting and stopped where I was working in Hudson to tell me. I left work and drove to the pasture and saw Liberty struggling to stand up in the irrigation canal. His legs were entwined in the sheep and barbed wire that had been parts of the fence along the ditch. A barbed wire even stretched tight across his back. He was stuck in all the wire and couldn't get up. He thrashed violently until he heard and saw me, then he waited for me to help him. I was in the ditch with him, pulling and moving the wires, trying to get him loose. Blood was coming from so many places on him. How badly was he cut under the water was the scariest part of the whole situation.

I had no tools to cut the wires so I started to run home for fence pliers. Thinking I was leaving him, he began to thrash and try to get up. Crying loudly to him, I promised him I would be right back with tools. I couldn't look back as I flew down the road towards home. I wasn't gone but a few minutes, but by the time I stopped at the pasture gate, Liberty and Sandy were standing side by side on the ditch bank. Blood colored the water that was still running off Liberty and he was shivering uncontrollably. I don't know how long he had been in the water but I knew it was cold enough to put him in hypothermia.

As I led him to and out the gate, all of his family came along. All except the mustang girls. Try as they would to follow, the gelding cut them off and pushed them away. I put my horses in a neighboring corral and went back for the girls. Knowing Sassy would follow, I got a twine around Pricey and headed for the gate. That gelding wasn't going to let ME take her. He came at me with his ears back and tried to get between me and Pricey. I shouted and screamed, threw rocks and sticks, and finally was able to get the girls out of the pasture. The gelding almost came through the fence gate after us. What a domineering animal he was, and, shamefully, what a terrible situation I had put my animals into.

I put the girls in with the rest of the family in a small, vacant pasture across the road and took Liberty out. Walking him along with the vehicle, something I had trained all of horses to do, we eventually got home and I loaded him into the trailer. By that time, Liberty had stopped shivering and most of the blood had clotted and stopped dripping. The vet said most of the cuts were superficial and would heal soon. He treated the worst areas and assured me the walk home had helped stop the hypothermia and any "stiffening" up that might have set in. The worst of the cuts had been in the genital area. The wires had sawed him quite a bit but not extremely deep. He was very lucky. He had just been doing his job, trying to take care of and protect his family.

11
NEW ADVENTURES

I attended a seminar in Dubois which involved all the Federal Agencies giving talks about trails in general. The Yellowstone National Park Service representative, Tom Oliff, was of special interest to me. Although I had enjoyed a number of pack trips through parts of Yellowstone National Park, Tom had touched on the subject of day riding park trails. I was able to have a one on one discussion with him about the riding I had done. He gave me lots of encouragement to try some park trail day riding

Along with some specifics, he gave me suggestions for references such as guide books available to help me decide where to ride. The first ride he suggested was an eight mile ride to Heart Lake. Also suggested was a forest service campground outside of the park boundary, which was perfect as no overnight camping is allowed at park trailheads. The trailhead was eleven miles north of the South Entrance. Paying my entrance fee, I reminded the attendant about the horse and trailer I was pulling. "Oh, you have a horse?" he asked. I guess he thought it was a different looking camper I was pulling. Although the parking area was small, the signage and trails are very horse friendly. It seemed strange that I didn't see any other horses that day, or for that matter, on any of my day rides in the park. Being a popular hiking trail was not a problem, everyone I met was as happy to be there as I was.

I was very confident that Liberty would handle the new situations we would encounter with his usual cautious, positive attitude. He didn't disappoint me in the least. We passed trees with bear claw scratches on them and scat on the trail which caused him to stop and smell. His alertness increased but there was no hesitation in his step as we continued on our way. Beautiful, pristine blue pools caught my attention. As we neared some bubbling mud pots, I heard him smelling the new scents. He looked intently at steaming vents in barren areas. Only when we approached a newly constructed wooden bridge over a small creek did he hesitate and seem unsure, looking from side to side to decide where best to go. Hot, mud pots bubbled on both sides of the bridge. Backing up a couple steps, I let him stand and make his decision, then I asked him to go forward. As we stepped on the bridge I felt the heat rising from the water. Slowly he walked over the bridge as if evaluating each step.

It was a totally new experience and I let him learn about all of it at his own speed. The next times we crossed hot water areas he hardly even reacted at all to them. Dropping down to the lake, we found a nice area where he could munch some grass while I enjoyed my pack lunch. He was not interested in the least in drinking from the lake or even creeks running into the lake. I learned later that pack mules will drink from the lake. There was no fresh water for Liberty. He didn't eat that much grass, maybe it smelled or tasted funny. We rode for a ways down the trail and part way around the small lake before turning around to head back. Later, I learned the trail is part of the CDT through Yellowstone National Park. There are campsites along the trail, some of which are designated horse camps, but all must be reserved in advance and camping is strictly regulated and enforced. Day riding worked for me. A whole new doorway to adventure had opened.

My next park trail ride was across the road from the Heart Lake trailhead. The park representative was the back country trail coordinator and he had personally hiked many of the areas he suggested. I had called him and told him about the enjoyable and successful first ride. He happily suggested the Lewis Lake Channel Trail to Shoshone Lake that circles back to the trailhead as the Dogshead Trail. Later, I learned that the portion of the trail between the lakes is not recommended because it is not maintained.

I am so glad that he told me about it because I came to a point on the trail along the river channel where the water travels away and back in a big horseshoe. A giant rock sits in the water at the top of the bend. The picture I have is beautiful but in no way does justice to the quiet beauty of the spot. I sat horseback for a long time before I could get myself ready to go on. It's just one of those places you feel so content at and you wish you could take it with you. I have. It's right there in my memories.

Liberty waited patiently, then we continued on. There were some tricky places to negotiate but my trustworthy boy got us through. The portion of the trail that heads back to the parking area is basically an old abandoned road bed. Occasionally, you are on road tread, but the quiet surroundings make for an enjoyable experience. Arriving back at the trailer, Brandy was happy to see us. (She couldn't go with us as dogs aren't allowed in the back country). A park ranger pulled in as I unsaddled and we had a great visit. He told me about the channel trail not being recommended because it wasn't maintained. When I told him how much I enjoyed the ride, he was pleased Tom had recommended it. I was having such an enjoyable time telling the ranger about my ride, he had to remind me to keep my dog nearby. She was busy sniffing everything and I hadn't put her on the leash and kept her under my control. He laughed as he reminded me. My euphoria was very apparent.

I returned to the Heart Lake trail a number of weeks later. I had been camping and riding at the Double Cabins trail head area and I decided I would drive up to the forest campground south of the Yellowstone border. After spending the night I awoke to anticipation of a pleasant ride in the area. A truck pulling a horse trailer entered the campground and I stepped out to visit the occupants. They were from Missouri, and had been riding trails in Teton National Park and south of Jackson. They were eager to learn about new ones.

I told them about my rides in Yellowstone Park and they were interested. After some discussion and pouring over my maps and Yellowstone Trails book, off we all headed for Yellowstone. It was cloudy, windy, and threatening rain so we decided on the Heart Lake Trail. The trip in was enjoyable and their horses were willing, although apprehensive. A short lunch time at the lake due to the onset of rain soon had us headed back out.

The trail was literally ours and we quickly trotted along. The "walker" horses they had made for a fast pace and they apologized for me having a hard time keeping up. Laughingly, I assured them we were having no problem. My Liberty trotted right up behind them and I could stay right with him comfortably. Arriving back at the trail head, we exchanged information and vowed to stay in touch, but, sadly, we didn't. I'm sure they enjoyed their Yellowstone horseback experience and would relive the memories. Perhaps some day they returned and experienced more day rides in the park.

I returned to Heart Lake another time and found there had recently been a large landslide and blow down of trees across a long section of the trail. My jaw dropped as I topped over the ridge and looked down the trail to the lake in the distance. Mother Nature can be ferocious and her fury and destruction were tremendous. A new trail had been scratched through the jumble of downed trees. We rode down the mountain to the lake but the terrain and vistas definitely looked different. Even the pools and creeks had changed. They were not serene and clear as they had been. I wondered what the resident wildlife's reactions to this change in their habitat would be. Even Liberty seemed to notice the difference. He was very alert but didn't hesitate anymore than he had on previous visits.

Later, a tragic occurrence took place in the same area. A park biologist and his volunteer helper were killed in a smaller land slide. Tom had planned to join them at the site but he was delayed by personal circumstances. What a sad memory for him.

I was ready for new adventures. The next trail I would check out was one that went up into Pelican Valley. My park friend cautioned me to be sure I discussed my planned ride with the ranger at the Lake/Fishing Bridge Ranger Station. As I pulled into the parking lot my horse trailer ended up with the open area above the doors facing a large bison grazing on the lawn. Liberty looked back and seemed fascinated by the buffalo and I wondered what he thought it was. It didn't seem to scare him, he just stared intensely. The great animal wasn't bothered in the least by our presence, and it continued with it's eating. The brief view and scent of this strange animal would help prepare Liberty for encounters down the trail.

Discussing my intended ride in the Pelican Valley to the northeast, I learned a lot of interesting information from the ranger. A fire was in progress but an early morning monitoring showed it not to be threatening the area I would be in. Many of the trails that headed out of the trailhead parking area were either closed in sections or had strictly enforced hours. You couldn't enter before 9:00 AM and must be back out at the trailhead by 7:00 PM, unless you were a through traveler and could make it to your reserved campsite by nightfall. Trailheads were checked. The enforcement was necessary because the trails went through prime grizzly bear habitat and the whole area was under designated bear management. Research and information gathering was conducted. Monitoring of bears and their activities was even done from Pelican Cone lookout sightings. The ranger cautioned me to read and obey any directives I came to.

My first intended route to explore was thwarted by a large sign saying "Trail closed due to bear activity". I didn't need to be told twice. It was the Turbid Lake trail. Not particularly interesting sounding anyway, according to my guide book, so we headed down the main Pelican Valley trail. The meadow is huge, with fingers of forest extending down into it, with the trail traveling through. The forest, which the fingers of trees jutted out from, was on up the mountainside on our right. Contrasting with the thick, dark, and quiet forest, the meadow was open, sunny, and noisy with birds and other small critters. It was a beautiful day for a ride.

As we entered the beginning of the first finger of trees, I noticed an increased alertness in Liberty. He was smelling the scents in the air and looking from one side to the other. His step slowed a bit but he continued on. We soon exited the trees and we walked on down the trail on the edge of the meadow. Going through longer distances in the trees, sometimes Liberty would start at a slower pace, pick up a little as we neared the midsection, then hurry to the end and out of the trees. He didn't like being in them at all. Some of the tree sections were short distances but we came to one that was long enough that we couldn't see the next open area ahead of us. Liberty slowed down considerably as we approached the first trees and eventually stopped. I let him stand and absorb the situation. He wouldn't enter the trees and it was making me apprehensive, too.

No way would I insist on him going forward if he was this convinced not to. We both looked all around. I couldn't see or hear anything out of the ordinary. What should I do? My old boy made his decision. He stepped to our left off the trail, and walked along and around the edge of the trees through the meadow until we came back to the trail where it exited out of the trees. How amazing he could be! Truly, I was just along for the ride.

I met and exchanged bits of information with several hikers. One couple had strong accents but we managed to find enough words to express ourselves. They told me there were buffalo at the river crossing, which was quite a long way according to the map. On down the trail we went. Small hills gave me views of the area they had mentioned and I could make out tiny dots near the water. Topping over a hill, I was totally startled by a large animal not very far ahead of us. Oh, my! A huge, shaggy buffalo was crossing the trail and we were way to close to him.

As we stood rooted in place, Liberty smelled the air and stared. I think he decided it was not a cow or moose but wasn't sure what it was. I kept him still and the big thing looked casually at us as it walked slowly across the trail and down into a small draw. I did have presence of mind to fish out my camera and snap a quick picture while we waited for him to move on. The disposable camera made the buffalo appear to be a long way off, but my pounding heart reminded me that we were in this big guy's space. Liberty kept his cool and as the animal ambled away, he, too, walked on.

I jabbered away about what had just happened and how much I loved my Liberty. What an incredible experience we had just been fortunate enough to have. The highly emotional reactions had drained me physically as well as mentally. After riding a ways down the trail, I decided I was ready to turn around.

We passed through the draw where the buffalo had crossed the trail. He had moved on and was no where to be seen. That was okay by me. One close encounter was enough for the time being. Thankfully, it had been positive.

On down the trail we walked and on into the fingers of trees the trail went across. We approached the lengthy route that Liberty had bypassed. I didn't cue him at all and he entered the trees. I was looking everywhere, as was Liberty. I could hear him smelling the air and I caught the same strong scent. Probably a bear had been bedded down nearby or crossed the trail recently, perhaps even marked the surroundings with his scent. Liberty's behavior had convinced me. Now, he was totally agreeable to passing through, although his pace quickened as we caught sight of the meadow again. It certainly had been a place I didn't want to linger in. Possibly, the perceived threat, whatever it was that unnerved both of us, had moved further on up into the thick forest.

The balance of that day's ride was uneventful. The scenery was gorgeous and I took many pictures. The fire was quite a distance away and didn't show up very good but I snapped a few of it anyway. In the distance I saw some firefighters on a hill monitoring the fire. I had not been in any danger, but I was thankful for the information given to me. If I had been able to continue on up the Pelican Creek Trail, I eventually could have intersected with the Lamar River Trail and the area Gordie and I had visited years before. It really wasn't that far distance wise, but, it would have been a full fledged pack trip involving reserved campsites, etc. I wasn't looking for a pack trip experience at that point. Day rides were totally filling my capacity for enjoyable park outings.

Because I had ridden on so much of the CDT in Wyoming, the Yellowstone Park sections were of major interest to me. I signed up for and participated on several Alliance trail building projects. Most of the projects included camping privileges and I wasn't able to bring my horse. I was able to mentally tie the route through the park together, but, I wondered how it would go through the highly congested tourist areas. The trail crossed the highway north of Old Faithful and the apparent route west went right through Biscuit

Basin, a large basin of Geysers, and on down the Summit Lake Trail. I was really perplexed on how equestrians, and other travelers with animals, would reach the start of the Summit Lake Trail without going across the geyser basin on the board walks.

Park personnel at the visitor center didn't know much about the CDT and no work projects had been done in that immediate area. Someone told me about a person that might have some information but he was on time off. That person was connected with a crew that rode horses and did work on the trails for the park. An "abandoned as well as unusable" trail went from Old Faithful to the beginning of the Summit trail west of the geysers but I was told it definitely should not be attempted. I wasn't able to reach my park service friend, so I would have to make my own decisions, much as any unsuspecting, CDT long distance traveling, person would.

Arriving at the parking area for Biscuit Basin, I had to circle around a couple times to find a place to park. Although it was later in the tourist season, this popular site had lots of people viewing the various geysers, mud pots, and pools. Steam erupted from many fissures and rocks of every color were strewn about. The large area was accessible using a series of boardwalks.

To reach the Summit Trail on the west side of the geyser basin, we began our walk over the Fire Hole River bridge. We stepped onto the boardwalk, much to the surprise of people coming towards us. I decided I would have better control of Liberty by riding him rather than by walking in front of him. As we neared the first walkers, some just walked on by us and others were not sure what to do and some looked back as if to turn around. I smiled the whole time, greeted each one, and told the apprehensive ones to just stop and stand quietly on their side as we passed by them. Some children were excited to see a horse, especially HERE, and I asked them pleasantly not to reach out.

A number of cameras clicked and I'm sure we were on video at least twice. We slowed as we neared sitting benches where the boardwalk was wider and people could stand back from us. One elderly oriental woman clutched a small child close to her as we approached. I smiled as big of a smile as I could and told her they were fine. The poor woman looked horrified but the child had a huge smile on her face. Only one person commented loudly that a horse shouldn't be on the boardwalk. I ignored him and concentrated on smiling. Passing an intersection where another boardwalk headed north, some people even hurried to get closer to say hello and ask where we were headed for. I answered by telling them this was the only way for me to get on the Summit Trail.

Liberty's previous experience around the thermal features of Heart Lake was serving us well. The concentration of features in this area was the biggest difference. He didn't mind traffic or crowds. Granted, he eyed each individual thermal site intensely, but continued on without hesitation. What an experience it was. When we reached the end of the boardwalk and stepped back on solid ground, I let loose a huge sigh of exhilaration, and Liberty dropped his head and began munching the tall grass on the side of the trail. He seemed to be saying "all in a day's work, now let's eat." I dismounted, stepped away from the trail to have a drink of water and snack, and reflect on what we had just done.

Still shaking my head and grinning to myself, we resumed our travel. An off shoot trail went a short distance to Mystic Falls but I wanted to continue on the Summit Trail. We entered trees and never got to any open areas so presently it was time to turn around. We met only one couple and the trail supposedly was pretty much the same all the way to Summit Lake and on to the Idaho border, not that far distant.

All the way back through the quiet of the forest, my mind kept jumping forward to the activity and surroundings at the geyser basin. Thinking positive thoughts kept my anticipation on an even keel. We walked out of the trees and approached the boardwalk. It was straight ahead for a few feet, then it made a right angle and turned directly back to the left in a dog leg fashion, then straight on.

We had just gotten past the dog leg part and were facing the other end and bridge area when Liberty hesitated, stopped totally, looked ahead, then began to back up. I stopped him and urged him forward but he backed further and on to the dog leg. I guided him as best I could and he soon stopped. When we were back on the ground, I got off and tried to figure out what was wrong. He stood there staring ahead and I began to hear a sound and realized what had changed. A geyser near the boardwalk and almost all the way on the other side was beginning to spurt steam and boiling water and as we watched, it increased in intensity. Spraying many feet in the air, onlookers giggled and hurried on so as not to get wet from the eruption.

The spray and steam steadily dissipated, but before it did, I had presence of mind to snap a quick picture with both Liberty and the eruption visible. When it had stopped totally, I mounted up. We walked quietly down the boardwalk, past the signed geyser location, which I had previously missed seeing in my preoccupation with pedestrians, and on over the bridge into the parking lot area. He did not hesitate anywhere on the return trip across the boardwalk, even as we passed the now quiet geyser. He had sensed it was no longer a questionable threat.

As I unsaddled him, I stopped numerous times to hug and kiss his neck and face. Again, he had given me some remarkable experiences. We had accomplished them in a safe manner, thanks to the trust that existed between us. This latest adventure was not for the faint of heart, nor the inexperienced, whether it be animal or rider. What we had just done could have had a turn of events and been disastrous. Even though the boardwalk was wide enough to turn an animal around on, any misstep off on either side would have resulted in terrible burns and possibly even death. Some areas had side hand rails but there was much open boardwalk. A balking or runaway animal could have caused unmentionable circumstances.

This part of the CDT was a place waiting for an accident to happen. It was UNSAFE for stock use and there was no viable alternative other than exiting the park and avoiding the area altogether. Missing this mysterious, intriguing area would be unfortunate for the CDT traveler with stock. Leaving the parking lot, I stopped again at the nearby visitor center and voiced my concern. I was able to talk to a park person that told me a trail crew was looking at the "abandoned" trail as a future work project. Driving home, I decided I needed to carry this further. Several phone calls to the Alliance didn't produce anything other than "we'll look into it". I wrote some letters, also, but I haven't ever seen any geyser basin work projects scheduled by them. I have not followed up on the situation.

My horses had become a very close knit family. When they were all up at the pasture by my house, I always knew if one of them was out loose and wandering. The rest would raise such a racket or the whole bunch would find a way out to go, too. If I had to find them, generally they were all together or close by. Normally, I would catch up Liberty and lead him along with the vehicle I was driving and the rest would tag along. If they got out of a pasture elsewhere around town, they ate their way back home.

I got into a routine of taking Liberty down to the corner where a vacant corner lot behind a building had pretty good munchies, especially before or after the growing season. He would eat until he had enough and then begin heading back home, turning into my driveway, walking to the gate, and waiting for me to come put him back in the pasture. Sometimes I would take him out of the pasture and let go of him while I was closing the gate. Off he would go, walking down to the corner and start munching. Even if none of his family was there, he knew where to go.

I remember several times I woke up to find my bunch had gotten out of another pasture and they all were back home and in their pasture because the gate was open, and there they were, waiting for me to feed them. I didn't relish waking up to the sound of numerous hooves clattering OUT the driveway in the dark but it did happen occasionally over the years. Why in the heck did it happen more often in the winter, more often than not, as the temperature went below freezing and snow swirled? As close to the highway as I was, thankfully, they didn't get up on it and cause an accident, or be hit and killed or injured.

Liberty benefited by the friendship of my neighbor, Joe. With advancing age came inability to chew hay and the resulting weight loss. He could get along with the addition of a ration of Equine Senior made by Purina, but he still wanted to graze. As the growing season passed, hay became the feed. Joe noticed that Liberty seemed to not be able to eat what the others ate and started letting Liberty come through the gate into his yard to nip off the tips of the lawn grass. The front teeth were okay for doing this as the grass had been well tended by Joe all summer. It wasn't unusual to see Liberty over by Joe's fence, head hanging over it, and hear a whinny when he spotted Joe. Sometimes, I would look out the window and see all the horses in Joe's yard, with Joe standing nearby, a big grin on his face. I think he particularly loved Liberty, but he was so good to all of the horses. We all missed Joe and his wife when they sold their place and moved.

On a particularly nice fall day, I loaded Liberty and Sassy into the horse trailer and drove to the Bruce's campground and parking area. When we headed up Fairfield Hill, both of them had lots of energy and seemed to enjoy the walk, stopping for short breathers along the way up. I enjoyed the views as we topped up and into the trees on the trail to Squaw Creek crossing.

We passed the junction of the trail cut off that goes across and down to the Middle Fork trail. We continued toward the Squaw Creek. A friend had told me you could ride to Shoshone Lake this way. I had seen the trail on the map but someone else had said they had gone that way while on a hunting trip and had gotten into terrible terrain with bogs, disappearing trail, and, of course, lots of downfall and other obstacles. I decided we would only go until we ran into any difficulties, then turn around. I was anxious to see how far we would get.

On down the trail we went, enjoying the beautiful weather. A deer tripped quietly through the trees, not particularly bothered by us or us by it. We passed a falling down, rotting, log building. I don't know how far we got. We never lost the trail or got into any great difficulty but, presently I decided we had reached a nice area to stop and have a bite in a small, pleasant, open meadow. The horses enjoyed some bites of grass and I ate snacks from my pommel pack, and then we turned around and headed back.

The timing would bring us back to the trailer before dusk. About half way back, the sun was beginning to set over the mountains behind us. We saw more deer as we neared the face of Fairfield Hill. Coming out of the trees was a good feeling. Down the steep grade we walked, passing the familiar trail junction to Shoshone Lake. The trail levels off and then the switch backs begin. Liberty began to stop, at first only occasionally, then more frequently.

At first, I didn't press him to go on but soon he was stopping often, sometimes after only ten or fifteen feet. He wasn't very anxious to go on. It wasn't that he wanted to eat along the way, he just didn't want to move. I got off and led him but soon he was stopping again. I put the bridle on Sassy, jumped on her bare back, and walked on with her. Tears filled my eyes as he stood and looked at me. Of course, I wouldn't leave him. I turned Sassy around and went back to him.

After waiting awhile, I started out again. Liberty would follow a ways, then stop. At least he was moving and deciding when to go on. Sassy slowly picked her way down, Liberty falling behind, then catching up as we stopped and waited for him. Nearing the bottom, I was suddenly surprised to notice Liberty on our side and passing us! Down the trail he went, gradually increasing his pace. Whatever his discomfort had been, it had eased and he seemed his normal self. Totally happy for him, I still didn't want to have him loose ahead of me. As we neared the parking area, I urged Sassy around him and caught up his lead rope. It was good to be back at the trailer.

Turning the events over in my mind, I decided Liberty had experienced a form of "tying up". It is a painful condition caused by a number of things. Trailer hauling a long distance, lack of sufficient drinking, improper conditioning, extreme exertion, and many more causes exist. Probably, Liberty had worked too hard going up and then the difficulty of coming down had brought on the condition. I had done the right thing by letting him decide when he could go on. Pain had eased as time passed and he didn't aggravate the situation by trying too hard. We were fortunate that he had recovered as quickly as he did. None the less, I wouldn't have left him.

My quarter horses have been blessed with long, healthy lives. When Missy was 27, she, like her mother, Babe, had reached the advanced stages of arthritis. Able to get around okay, she stayed close to Liberty or off by herself so the others wouldn't run her around. One day I noticed her walking around Liberty with a staggering pace. Something was wrong.

I called the vet and was told to bring her in. As I approached her, she staggered sideways and went down. She was able to get back up and I led her to the trailer. With great hesitation she started to get in but went down again part way in. It was so terrible to watch her trying to get up. As she got back on her feet outside the trailer, I told her it was okay and turned her loose. She went slowly back to Liberty. I called the vet back but he was unable to come so suggested I end the misery of her apparent strokes by getting someone nearby to put her down. I led her away from Liberty and she went down again.

After my neighbor did what he had to do, it was a touching scene to see each of the horses walk slowly over to her, put their head down close for a moment, then move away. As Sassy approached, it occurred to me that she might strike out at Missy as she often did. I was ready to stop her if she did but, again, it was that moment of tenderness and respect. It broke my heart but ended the tragic situation for both me and Missy.

Being aware of the impending loss of Liberty, every moment spent with him was precious. We took slow walks during which I reminisced over the memories we had shared. There were so many. Sometimes I sat quietly by him, thankful for all the memories, whether good or not. He had such a warm sound with his sweet, low voice. It always made me smile and I can hear it now in my mind.

In his advanced age, he was losing his hearing. His appetite and eyesight remained good and with regular exercise, he was in good shape. To ensure his getting his special senior feed, we developed a system. If I was within sight of the horses, he would watch me. If the other horses heard me or saw me, he reacted to them, then looked for me. Watching me intently, my action determined his response. If I swung my arm up and around in a "come here" motion, he came. If I did nothing, he looked away or resumed grazing. When he came to eat, he entered the corral and I closed the gate behind him so the others couldn't enter and eat his feed, which he really didn't object to sharing.

Because I didn't hook the gate, when he was finished, he just pushed the gate open and walked out to join the others. The system worked for us. If they were in a different pasture, I stayed by him to keep the others away. I enjoyed those quiet moments with him.

Liberty turned 31, a ripe old age, and still enjoyed vitality and good health. We took walks to nearby grassy places. I spent as much time with him as possible. Then, one August day things changed. He didn't respond with his usual interest. As he walked toward me, his head low, eyes vacant and dull, nothing seemed right about him. In the next few days, he was more distant and lifeless. Although he was eating and drinking, it was so much slower and eventually he would stand for long periods before taking another bite.

The day that I saw him walk with a halting step right into the rear side of Sandy was the sign that he too, like Missy, was having strokes and wouldn't get better. He walked on and around and through the horses as if he was lost and didn't know where to go. My heart broke with such pain as I made the decision to call the vet and make arrangements. I always knew it was coming but it hurt so much now that it had.

The day the vet came, I sat with Liberty, hugging his neck and telling him with my tears and words how much he meant to me and how he would always be alive in my heart and mind. His spirit would live on. And so he has. I helped him transition through his "senior years". He is helping me through mine with memories and the writing of this story of our shared experiences over 30 years.